EMPTY HOUSE

Acknowledgements

Il Chun Sunim for advice on the Korean Zen Tradition
The gracious and hospitable monks of the featured temples
Ebony Cameras Ltd.
Professor Seok Chul Kim of Archiban
Professor Kevin O' Rourke
Timothy Savage of Nautilus
The librarians at Dongguk University, Seoul
Tibor Balogh for photo selection
Rupert Atkinson for proofreading
And with special thanks to Ian Wilson for text editing, photographic expertise
and continuous assistance and encouragement, without which this book could
not have been finished

All photographs by the author except:

pp. 55, 64, 157, 240, 251, 267, 273, 275   Ian Wilson
pp. 124, 256   Dong Kun Kim
pp. 30, 44, 59, 123, 254   Sang Im Lee
pp. 231   Bo Ha Park
pp. 130, 131, 132   Yong Bae Ko

All calligraphy by:
Yoo Chon Lee Dong-ik
Hyang Chon Kim Yong-jik

Interviews with Zen master Jinjae, Patriarch Seo-ong, Zen master Seung Sahn
and Popjon Sunim conducted by Byong-Hwal Cho of the 'Bulgyo Shinmun'
(Buddhist Newspaper) and translated into English by Yonhee Chung and
Chris Verebes.

For the sake of consistency, the word "Zen" has been used throughout the text,
except where the context dictates otherwise. "Zen" is the Japanese
transliteration of the Chinese word "Ch'an" which is derived from the Indian
word, "Dhyana" meaning meditation or absorption. The Korean transliteration of
the word is "Son".

EMPTY HOUSE

Zen Masters and Temples of Korea

Chris Verebes

Eastward

Contents

Foreword by Wontaek Sunim

Buddhism was first transmitted to the Korean peninsula during the 'Three Kingdoms' period of Koguryo, Paekche, and Shilla. During the Unified Shilla period it was embraced as the official state religion. Since that time, Buddhism has done much to shape the development of Korean culture and over the years it has been intimately related to the fortune and destiny of the Korean people. Consequently throughout the country we still find many Buddhist temples in which have lived many eminent monks who have done much to enrich the spirit of the Korean people.

During the Unified Shilla and Koryo Dynasties, the importing of Buddhism from T'ang China contributed heavily to the creation of an advanced culture and social order. Buddhism however suffered a strong reversal of fortune during the Neo-Confucian Choson Dynasty, when it was oppressed by the state. It was gradually prohibited to enter monastic life, and the construction and renovation of temples became very difficult. Despite the endeavors of a number of great masters to propagate and keep the teachings alive during this period, Buddhism existed within a very narrow ambit. Nevertheless throughout this period of repression and even during the Japanese colonial period (1910~1945), Buddhism continued to make an enormous contribution to the development of the nation's culture and spiritual life.

During the mid 50's the reformation of Korean Buddhism began. Great strides were taken throughout the 60s, 70s, and 80s. Many temples were reconstructed and repaired, and the reformation of Buddhist cultural life was initiated. Furthermore, after many years of hardship, Buddhist aspirants began to show a renewed interest in seeking after the truth. Today, firmly based on the Buddhist teachings of the innate Buddha nature that everyone possesses and can realize through training of the mind, the Buddhist traditions of Zen meditation, Yombul (prayer), and Sutra reading (看經), are now enjoying a renaissance. Furthermore, in all temples throughout the country, the fundamental Buddhist principles of compassion towards all living beings (攝衆和合) and salvation (廣度衆生) are again being taught. Meanwhile since the 1990's, Korean Buddhism has gradually been achieving a higher profile and greater worldwide recognition. A number of Korean Buddhist masters have been teaching overseas and an increasing number of foreign students of Buddhism have been arriving in Korea to pursue studies here.

Nevertheless, despite Korea's long Buddhist history and the numerous eminent masters who have been produced on this soil, there still remains an insufficiency of well-written materials in English, which convey the true essence of the Korean Buddhist tradition. In this sense, coming at this time, the aptly titled Empty House should prove to be a very valuable reference to those with an interest in Zen Buddhism. No doubt it will also do much to contribute to the understanding of the hitherto, comparatively lesser-known, Zen (Son) tradition of Korea. To this end I would like to express my gratitude to the author who has been a student of Zen Buddhism for a number of years and personally visited and photographed the temples featured in this book. The result is an impressive work of depth and sincerity, which I believe captures the real spirit of the Korean tradition.

In addition to telling the story of the Korean Zen tradition, the book also includes recent interviews conducted with contemporary Zen masters who represent the living face of Korean Buddhism today. Altogether therefore, I expect that this book will play an important role in making the world of Korean Zen Buddhism known to the world, and will serve as an effective guide to those seeking to understand the Buddhist culture of Korea.

Wontaek Sunim | Director of General Affairs, Chogye order

Biography

Wontaek Sunim graduated from the department of political science at Yonsei University in 1967, and was ordained as a Buddhist monk at Haein-sa in 1972, receiving full Bhikku precepts at Pomo-sa in 1974. He became the Director of Paengnyon Buddhist Cultural Foundation in 1987, and the Chairman of the Buddhist Publication Association in 1990. He was an elected member of the 10th General Assembly, and since 1992 he has been the Director of General Affairs of the Chogye order.

Foreword by Oh Kwang Sunim

According to statistics, Buddhism is currently the "fastest growing religion in the West". In most Western countries, for example, the Dalai Lama is already a household name, and people who are interested in Buddhism can easily visit numerous Buddhist Centers and web-sites connected with Buddhism or go to hear public talks given by spiritual teachers from diverse Buddhist schools. Also, numerous Buddhist texts have been translated by scholars and many are readily available. Certainly Buddhism is no longer the arcane religion that it might once have been perceived to have been. At the philosophical/intellectual level, Buddhism has also had a far-reaching impact, although the exact extent of this influence is hard to ascertain. It would be fair to say that many concepts associated with Buddhism, such as karma and rebirth, have been absorbed, perhaps unconsciously, into the everyday vocabulary of life in the West. Furthermore, at the very frontiers of scientific investigation of the physical world, scientists are finding correlations with the Buddhist Madhyamaka teachings concerning the emptiness of phenomena.

Meanwhile in Asia, where Buddhism originated and evolved to its present form over its 2,600-year history, Buddhism is clearly on the decline. Often seen as an outdated, passive religion, burdened with traditionalistic attitudes and a particular kind of inertia, in many Asian countries, including Korea, Buddhism is losing its followers.

This book, therefore, with its photographs of Korean temples and biographical information about the most famous of the Korean Zen Masters, will hopefully provide some insight into the lesser-known Korean Zen tradition.

Buddhism deals with life. The reality of our lives involves suffering. This is quite obvious, particularly when we look around us at the world of today. The Buddhist teachings invite us to investigate our lives in order to understand and remove the causes of suffering. This approach, which is usually considered to be pessimistic, is actually very realistic. Because of the emphasis that Buddhism lays on each individual's own efforts to understand and free him/herself from unnecessary suffering, it is actually both realistic and engaging. No religion as an institution, no church, or guru, can be in itself a solution. Not relying on any external power or grace, we are asked to turn within, and through reflection, meditation and insight, attain that same state of liberation that the Buddha Shakyamuni attained. This aspect of Buddhism is very attractive to many Westerners who are looking for a meaningful religion based primarily on reason and experimentation. Once the suffering is fully understood and cut through, once realization is attained, is that the end of the Buddhist path?

If it were, then the criticism of Buddhism as too hermetic and passive, and irrelevant to the modern world, would perhaps be correct. However, the Great Vehicle (Mahayana) Buddhism stresses that real enlightenment is never for oneself. It is enlightenment for all beings. This is because at the moment of enlightenment, the barrier between myself and others disappears forever.

On a functional level, a realized person still recognizes his name and takes care of his body, but the fundamental delusion based on the belief in a "Me versus Other" has vanished forever. A deluded person feels that he/she is a separate entity and therefore lives in fear of death. In the expectation of pleasure, he/she seeks self-protection, worries over the future and even envies the better fortune of others. However, a realized person is free of such delusions. Seeing the emptiness of all phenomena and thus all beings, he/she can identify him/herself with each and every sentient being. His/her mind is without fear or desire. It resembles an empty mirror that reflects everything that appears in front of it. It sees things exactly as they are. This being the case, the realized person can respond appropriately according to the needs of others. Free from the passions that obscure the mind's clarity, he/she always finds the most suitable way to help those who are in distress.

His activity is neither contrived nor forced, and since it comes from the place of complete freedom and clarity, it is compassionate and spontaneous. It is not fixed in any way. So drinking tea and staring through the window at the rain; even this becomes the act of a bodhisattva and saves beings from suffering.

Chinese Zen Master Lin Chi's favorite advice to his students was: "Become a man who does nothing!" The Mahayana Buddhist vow, that monks and nuns in Korea recite every morning, says, "Beings are innumerable; I vow to save them all." Paradoxically, these two statements seem to contradict each other. However, Lin Chi's man who does nothing is simply a man whose actions are not motivated by personal desires. So he may ceaselessly work for others, from morning to night, yet he does not even move his feet. He has attained what the Taoist would call "No-action action" or "doing through non-doing".

The great vow to save innumerable beings can never be fulfilled by an unenlightened person. It is not a vow arising from our subjective idea of changing the world. It arises from understanding the insubstantial, empty nature of the world, and from the perception that beings are suffering while living in their own dreams. The only way to save them is actually by helping them to wake up. So this is why any action of a being who is free from delusion becomes an opportunity for others to wake up and seek that same state of freedom.

Let us then examine the Korean Zen tradition as presented in this book, and let's ponder over the significance of the teachings that are included. And, most importantly, let's try to practice and attain the path of the Bodhisattva; the path of the peaceful warrior who attacks no one, except the delusion of which we are essentially composed.

Oh Kwang Sunim

Biography

Oh Kwang Sunim was born in Yugoslavia in 1962, and was ordained as a Buddhist monk in 1989. Initially ordained in the Zen tradition, he spent a number of years engaged in ascetic meditation practice in the Therevadan forest traditions of Thailand and Sri Lanka before arriving in Korea in 1998. He is currently a student of Zen master Seung Sahn.

Author's Note

In Korea today there are all together somewhere in the region of five thousand or more Buddhist temples and hermitages scattered across this small mountainous country, many of which are located in the most sublime and beautiful natural settings. Not all by any means are associated with the practice of Zen Buddhism. In fact, it would be more accurate to say that those temples in which Zen meditation is actively cultivated are the exception rather than the rule. Most likely it has always been this way and always will be. Due to the constraints involved in compiling this book, therefore, I have been forced to select only those temples which I feel have been most relevant to the unfolding history of Zen in this country. I would like to say from the outset, therefore, that this book is not intended as an exhaustive study of either Korean temple history, Buddhist history, or even Korean Zen for that matter. I would hope, though, that it would serve as a useful layman's guide to those with an interest in the Korean Zen tradition.

Essentially, what I've endeavored to do in this book is to present a simplified chronology of Zen in this country from its origins to the present day, by way of the Zen Masters who have been most influential in shaping the Korean Zen tradition. Since history is never played out in a vacuum but is always connected with actual geographic places that continue to exist well beyond the lifespan of history's protagonists, I've linked the Masters to the temples with which they were most closely associated during their lifetimes. Consequently, the sequence in which the temples appear in this book does not necessarily reflect the dates when the temples were established.

So here, in the pages that follow, are some of the Zen temples where dozens of generations of Zen monks and masters have lived, studied and trained in their quest for self-realization, over a period of more than 1,500 years. Some of the temples presented are no longer functional and have long since existed only as ruins, whilst others although existing structurally, serve only as museums of the past. However, in a few of these temples the spirit of the Zen tradition still lives on, and monks continue to live and train and seek self-understanding in much the same way as they did one thousand years ago.

Chris Verebes, November 2001

Introduction

Buddhism arrived in China from India during the 1st Century AD and was gradually transmitted to the Korean Peninsula from the 4th Century onwards. During that period the Korean Peninsula was divided into three kingdoms: Koguryo in the north, Shilla in the east and Paekche in the southwest. Shilla was the last of these three kingdoms to accept Buddhism as its official state religion in 527 AD.

In 660 AD, with the help of T'ang Dynasty China, Shilla conquered Paekche and Koguryo, and in 668 AD succeeded in unifying the peninsula. The period of the Unified Shilla Dynasty (668-935), which roughly corresponded with the T'ang Dynasty in China[1], saw the flourishing of Buddhism under the patronage of the state.

During this period many Korean monks travelled to China to study, returning with Buddhist scriptures and artifacts. Masters such as Chajang (see p.28), Wonhyo (see p.40) and Uisang (see p.46), contributed to the spread of the Buddhist teachings and the establishment of the doctrinal foundations of the main schools of Buddhism. The most influential of these schools was the Hwaom School established by Uisang, which was centered around Pusok-sa (see p.46). This period also saw the establishment of many of the largest and most important temples in the country, such as Bulguk-sa (see p.26), T'ongdo-sa (see p.28), Haein-sa (see p.62), and

Popchu-sa (see p.200), and the laying down of the institutional framework of the religion.

Zen[2] Buddhism was first introduced to Korea around 630 AD by Master Pomnang, who is reputed to have studied under the Fourth Patriarch[3]. It was not until later, however, that Zen began to take root in Korea. During the 9th Century the "sudden enlightenment" teachings developed by the Sixth Patriarch Hui-neng's[4] (638-713) Southern School began to arrive in Korea. Starting with Master Toui, a number of Korean monks who had studied under various successors of the famed Ma-tsu (709-788), returned to Shilla and established the so-called Nine Mountains Schools of Zen[5]. The flowering of Zen in Korea therefore roughly coincided with the "Golden Age of Zen" in China[6].

The Shilla Dynasty was replaced by the Koryo Dynasty in 935 AD. Nevertheless, the country's fortunes were still identified with Buddhism, and so the religion continued to prosper under state patronage. The Koryo Dynasty (935-1392) roughly corresponded with the Sung Dynasty (960-1297) in China, which saw the formalization and systematization of the dynamic and creative energy of the early Zen movement. Likewise in Korea, as the Nine Mountains Schools became politically more powerful, the vitality and spirit of the early years began to dissipate. During the late 12th Century however, Zen Master Chinul (1158-1210) (see p.114), regarded as Korea's most influential Buddhist thinker, did much to reinvigorate the Zen tradition. Also during this period, the original Nine Mountains Zen Schools were merged into one by Zen Master T'aego[7].

With the collapse of the Koryo Dynasty and its replacement by the Neo-Confucian Choson Dynasty (1392-1910), the fortunes of Buddhism began to wane. By the 16th Century Buddhism was being severely repressed, and from 1623 onwards monks were even prohibited from entering the capital. Just as it had in China in the wake of the Hui-cheng persecution of Buddhism in the 9th Century[8], Zen retreated into the mountains. In spite of these trials, masters such as Sosan (see p.174) and Samyong (see p.182) managed to keep the tradition alive.

Finally, towards the end of the Choson Dynasty, the state began to lift its oppressive policies, and from 1895 monks were once again allowed to enter the capital. This period saw a renewal of energy within the Zen community and the appearance of a number of eminent teachers such as Kyongho (see p.216), who did much to inspire the reformation of the Zen tradition. A new threat emerged, however, in the form of

Japanese imperialism. With the formal annexation of Korea by Japan in 1910, the Colonial government attempted to absorb Korean Zen into the Japanese Soto Zen tradition, but these attempts were vigorously resisted by the Korean sangha.

In the aftermath of the Japanese Colonial Period (1910-1945) and the Korean War (1950-53), the Korean Zen tradition has shown considerable resilience. In the face of all the social and political turmoil of the 20th Century, a number of influential masters have left their mark on the modern landscape. Significantly, masters such as Kusan (see p.250) and Seung Sahn (see p.279) have also been instrumental in transmitting the teachings to the West.

During the last decade, perhaps as a backlash to the widespread materialism that has swept through Korean society as the country has struggled to modernize, there has been something of a resurgence of interest in Zen Buddhism. Much work has gone into reconstruction and expansion of temples, and many Zen halls have either been re-opened or newly constructed. It is therefore with a renewed sense of optimism and hope that the Korean Zen establishment looks to the future as we step into the 21st Century.

Zen Masters and Temples of Korea

Bulguk-sa

Temple of the Buddha Land

The imposing Bulguk-sa temple complex stands on the western slopes of Mt. Toham on the outskirts of Kyongju, which was once the capital of the Shilla Dynasty (57 BC - 935 AD). As the name "Temple of the Buddha Land" implies, the temple was created to symbolize the Lotus Land of the Avatamsaka Sutra.

The temple was originally constructed on a small scale around the year 528 AD by King Pophung (r.514-540) for his mother Lady Yongje, and was called Pomnyu-sa. It was King Pophung's own conversion that largely paved the way for the acceptance of Buddhism in Shilla. It is said that in 528 AD King Pophung issued a decree that people should cease from killing living beings. Then in 535 AD he began to build a temple called Hungnyun-sa in Kyongju. When it was almost complete, he adopted the Buddhist name Popkong, meaning "Dharma Emptiness", and went to live there himself.

In 574 AD, Pomnyu-sa was expanded by Lady Chiso, the mother of King Chinhung (r.540-576), who officially adopted Buddhism as the state religion of Shilla. In 751 AD, during the reign of King Kyongdok (r.742-765), Prime Minister Kim Taesong began reconstruction work on Pomnyu-sa.

According to legend, Kim Taesong's birth into the Prime Minister's family was announced by a mysterious voice, and it was to honour his parents that he had the temple completely redesigned on a magnificent scale. Seventeen years later the completed temple was renamed Bulguk-sa. At the time of its completion it consisted of about two hundred wooden buildings arranged around a series of cloistered courtyards, each of which symbolically represented different aspects of the teachings of the Avatamsaka Sutra.

T'ongdo-sa

Temple of Crossing Over

Master Chajang (608-686) was one of the most influential Buddhist figures of the mid-Shilla period. He was born into an aristocratic family and was married at an early age. After fulfilling his obligations to his family, he left his wife and children and went into the mountains alone to practise austerities. Hearing of Chajang's excellence, the king wished to appoint him as a minister. Messengers were sent to the mountains to invite him to the royal court, but each time Chajang declined to leave the mountains. Finally the king became angry and announced that Chajang would be executed if he did not accept the position. To this Chajang replied, "I would rather live one day keeping the Buddha's precepts than a hundred years violating them." Touched by Chajang's dedication to the way of the Buddha, the king sanctioned his choice of the hermit's life.

In 636 AD, Chajang, like most of the other eminent teachers of his time, travelled to T'ang China to deepen his understanding of Buddhism. There he studied under many of the famous Buddhist masters of the time, including Tu-shun (557-640), the founder of the Hua-yen school, and Tao-hsuan (597-667), the founder of the Vinaya School.

After seven years in China, he had a vision of a heavenly being who told him that his country was in great danger of invasion from neighbouring kingdoms. The deity advised Chajang to quickly return to Shilla and build a nine-storey pagoda for the protection of the country.

Chajang returned to Shilla in 643 AD, and with the assistance of Queen Sondok (r.632-647) he supervised the construction of an enormous nine-storey wooden pagoda at Hwangnyong-sa (the Temple of the Yellow Dragon). This pagoda towered over the capital of Kyongju, and was considered one of the wonders of the Shilla kingdom. Unfortunately, this magnificent temple was razed to the ground by the invading Mongol armies in the 13th Century.

In 646 AD, Chajang established T'ongdo-sa temple on Mt.
Yongch'uk. Chajang is said to have brought back with him
fragments of the Buddha's bones and teeth from T'ang China
and deposited them in this temple. T'ongdo-sa is thus regarded
as one of Korea's so-called "Three Treasures" temples,
representing in this case the Buddha. (The other two are Haein-
sa, which represents the Dharma, or teaching, and Songgwang-
sa, which signifies the Sangha, or community of monks.) The
Buddha's relics are stored in a Stupa on the Vajra (Diamond)
Platform that can be viewed through a window in the main
Buddha Hall. Consequently, the hall itself contains no statue of
the Buddha and in this respect is quite unique.

Chajang used to preach at T'ongdo-sa on the meaning of the
Buddhist precepts. This temple was also used for the formal
ordination of monks, a tradition that continues to the present
day. Chajang did much to develop and formalize the Buddhist
order in Shilla, and it is said that eighty percent of all
households in Shilla took the five precepts. At the height of his
fame Chajang wielded considerable political influence, and in
some ways it was he who was responsible for the conflation of
religion with the political life of the kingdom.

At T'ongdo-sa

Autumn hued Mt. Yongji.

Clouds fly high above the peak.

Moon rises in the valley;

How many have found sanctuary here?

An ocean of blue ice.

This world like a dream.

Reality knows neither present nor past;

Water always flows down the cliff face[9].

Kyongbong (1892-1982)

Shinhung-sa

Temple of the God s creation

During Chajang's stay in China, he is said to have gone to Mt. Odae to pray for seven days and nights before a statue of Manjusri, the Bodhisattva of Wisdom. On the seventh day, an old man appeared before him and handed him the robe and bowl of the Buddha. He told Chajang that there is an Odae Mountain in Shilla too, where Manjusri is always present, and that he should go back to Shilla and find this place. Later, as Chajang was leaving the mountain, a dragon appeared and told him that the old man was none other than Manjusri himself.

Towards the end of his life, perhaps realizing that he'd drifted away from the austere practices of his early days, Master Chajang left the capital Kyongju and travelled alone north to the Odae Mountains hoping to meet Manjusri. On the way, he stayed in the Sorak Mountains and founded a small temple called Hyangsong-sa in the year 652 AD.

Later, Master Uisang expanded the temple, moved it to its present location and renamed it Sonjong-sa in 701 AD. Like many of Korea's other Zen temples, it was destroyed during the Hideyoshi invasions of the late 16th Century, and burnt down again in 1642. In 1647 it was rebuilt and given its present name.

Over the years many famous monks practised there. Today there is a small Zen hall for meditation monks.

After his sojourn in the Sorak Mountains, Chajang continued on his pilgrimage to Mt. Odae to meet Manjusri, staying in several hermitages there. Unfortunately, he failed in his quest and died a cold and lonely death in the mountains.

O'o-sa

My Fish Temple

There were quite a number of rather eccentric and colourful Buddhist masters who lived during the Shilla period. One of these was Master Hyegong. He was the son of a female servant who was a messenger for a local nobleman. When he was young he had many mystical experiences, which led to his becoming a monk. For most of his life as a monk, he lived in a small temple called Pugae-sa which means "Temple with a Thatched Roof". According to legend, he used to wander through the streets with a basket slung over his shoulder singing and dancing. For this reason, his nickname was the "Basket Monk". One day he was invited to the inauguration ceremony of a new temple called Kumgang-sa. That day it rained heavily, but apparently his clothes remained entirely dry.

In his later years he went to live at O'o-sa, which had been founded some time during the late 6th Century. One of his visitors at this temple was the famous Master Wonhyo (see p.40). Master Wonhyo was at this time engaged in writing commentaries on various sutras and came to Hyegong for advice. One day whilst they were staying at the temple together, they each released a fish into a nearby stream, betting on which fish would swim the farthest. One of the fish swam

swiftly away but the other died. Each of the monks claimed the victor as his own. That is why the temple is called "My Fish" temple!

Master Hyegong was one of the most unusual monks of his time. It was widely known that he had attained enlightenment. It is even said that he died while levitating. After his cremation, numerous sarira were found amongst his ashes. As a monk, his eccentric conduct of dancing in the streets and drinking shows how intimate he was with the common people; a true bodhisattva of the times.

Another master living at that time with whom Wonhyo seems to have been familiar was Master Nangji. He might even have been one of Wonhyo's teachers. According to the <Samguk Yusa>, "The Records of the Three Kingdoms", Master Nangji was a monk with mysterious powers who used to read the Lotus Sutra.

One other contemporary of Master Hyegong was Master Taean (571-644). There is hardly any record of his life, but his character and appearance were quite extraordinary. He completely shunned the society of the wealthy and powerful, preferring to live in the market area of the town. He used to wander amongst the people hitting an iron bowl calling, "Taean, taean". This is why he was called Taean, which means "Great Peace".

Punhwang-sa

Temple of the Perfume Emperor

The royal temple Punhwang-sa was built in 634 AD and was situated next to the magnificent Hwangnyong-sa (Temple of the Yellow Dragon), the most important and largest temple of the Shilla kingdom. Ironically, whilst nothing at all remains of the extensive complex of Hwangnyong-sa today, the stone-brick pagoda of Punhwang-sa is still extant.

The monk most closely associated with this temple was Wonhyo (617-687), a legendary figure in the history of Korean Buddhism. From a young age, Wonhyo was considered to be an exceptionally bright student. He was ordained as a monk at the age of twenty. In 650 AD at the age of thirty-three he set out for T'ang China via the northern overland route with his close friend Uisang. Legend has it that one night during their travels, Wonhyo and Uisang were overtaken by a storm and had to take shelter. In the dark they found what they thought was a hut, where they spent the night. In the morning they discovered to their horror that they'd been sleeping in a tomb with bones and skulls scattered all around. The storm did not abate however, and so they were forced to remain in the tomb for a second night. This time though they were unable to rest for fear of ghosts.

This experience is believed to have provoked a major realization in Wonhyo. He contem-plated, "Why was I able to sleep so peacefully last night when I thought that this was a hut, yet now in exactly the same place I'm unable to rest?" Then, as he later wrote, he realized, "When a thought arises various conceptions arise; when a thought ceases, there is no difference between a hut and a tomb."[10] He saw that everything depends on mind and that the reality we believe we perceive is merely the product of our thoughts. For reasons which are not altogether clear, Wonhyo and Uisang never reached China and instead returned to Shilla.

After his return to Shilla, Wonhyo spent much of his time teaching and writing extensive commentaries on the sutras whilst residing at Punhwang-sa. He was the author of some 240 works, of which around thirty still remain, including a commentary on the Awakening of Faith.[11]

Kirim-sa

Jehtvana Temple

Kirim-sa, just outside of Kwangju, was founded as Imjong-sa in the year 643 AD by the Indian monk Kwangyu, who had come to teach in Shilla. A few years later, Wonhyo greatly expanded the temple and renamed it Kirim-sa. It became one of the several temples around Kyongju where Wonhyo used to teach.

Wonhyo was a syncretic thinker with a very broad understanding of Buddhism who tried to integrate all the schools of Buddhism from the standpoint of the one mind. He expounded on his theory of synthesis in his <Shimmun Hwajaeng Non> ("Treatise on the Harmonization of the Disputes between the Ten Schools"). At a time when many masters were expounding various mutually exclusive theories and systems of practice based on particular Buddhist texts, Wonhyo tried to explain the texts from the point of view of his own experience of realization. Central to his thought is the concept of the Tathagata-garba, the all-embracing self-existent mind ground. As Wonhyo wrote on the Mind-only doctrine of the Avatam-saka Sutra:[12]

"All dharmas originate from the mind and so they are false. When the mind arises various dharmas begin, and when the mind ends, all the dharmas also end.

The Universal Dharma (the mutual integration of all phenomena) embraces all things, and all things mutually enter into and mutually identify with each other. The whole world exists in a speck of dust as the speck of dust exists in the world. The infinity of time exists in the shortest moment as the shortest moment exists in infinite time. In this way all things in the world relate to each other. Big is in small and small is in big; and so it is with stillness and movement and the one and the many. Everything has mutual identity. This is the nature of the universal Dharma."[13]

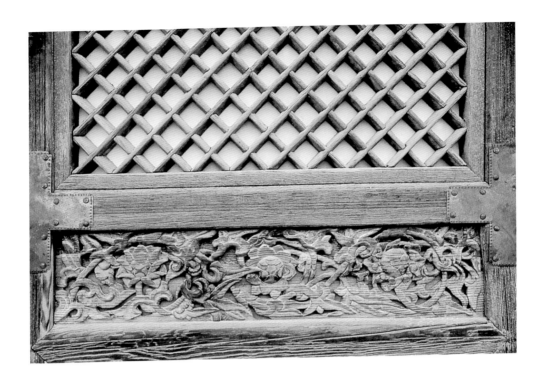

Towards the end of his life, Wonhyo left behind the orthodox
life of the monk and wandered freely throughout the country
mixing with and teaching the ordinary people by example.
Legend has it that he also fathered a son with a princess at the
royal court, who later went on to become one of the greatest
Confucian scholars in Shilla. After this event, he changed his
clothes to those of a layman and went by the name of Sosong
Kosa, meaning "unimportant layman". He would wander
through the villages and hamlets beating a gourd and chanting
a passage from the Avatamsaka Sutra: "Anyone who is not
disturbed by anything can transcend life and death instantly."
Although in the institutional sense he was not a Zen master, in
his spontaneity and depth of understanding he was perhaps the
greatest Zen master that the country has ever seen.

"The way people think is as different as south is from north, yet the Buddhist teachings remain the same from the past to the present. In seeking truth one clarifies reality, and through understanding phenomena one comes to recognize the noumena. Through exploration of the unfathomable one eradicates delusion; through abandoning one's pre-conceptions and opinions one achieves wisdom. Having attachments creates disputes; freeing oneself from desire one attains the way.[14]

The wisdom of prajna is the way, yet in reality there is no such thing as either the way or absence of the way. Therefore there is no such thing as either enlightenment or non-enlightenment. Further, we should recognize that since ultimately phenomena are without any definable characteristics, it follows that there is nothing that is not phenomena. If there is actually neither phenomena nor absence of phenomena, then how can truth possibly be explained?"[15]

Wonhyo

Pusok-sa

Floating Rock Temple

Pusok-sa was built on the orders of the royal court by Master Uisang in 676 AD after he returned from China. Master Uisang (625-702) was born into an aristocratic family in 625 AD and became a monk at an early age. It was Master Uisang who attempted to go to China with Wonhyo by traveling to the north via Koguryo, but failed. It is probable that they were suspected of being spies from Shilla and were turned back. A few years later, in 661 AD, he received permission from the Shilla court to join the party of the T'ang envoy who was returning to China by ship.

Uisang remained in China for around ten years, studying under the greatest monks of the period. At Chung-nan Mountain south of the T'ang capital of Chang'an, he stayed at the monastery of Chih-yen, the second patriarch of the Hwa-yen School, studying under him for eight years and eventually receiving transmission from him. A fellow disciple was Fa-tsang (643-712), the third patriarch, who was responsible for systematizing the doctrines of the Hwa-yen school in China.

The story goes that when Uisang was in China, he met a young woman named Sonmyo who fell in love with him. When the time came for him to return to Korea, he went to her house to

let her know that he was leaving. Unfortunately she wasn't home, so he left a message for her. When she received the message, she raced down to the waterfront, only to see Uisang's ship already disappearing over the horizon. She was so distraught that she flung herself into the sea, whereupon she was transformed into a dragon that followed Uisang's ship back to Shilla to protect him.

When Uisang returned to Korea, using the principles of geomancy he selected this site in the Taebaek Mountains to build a temple from which to preach the Avatamsaka Sutra. At that time, however, there were bandits living in the area who opposed the construction of the temple. Legend has it that Sonmyo, now a dragon, levitated a huge rock into the air to

frighten the bandits, who promptly ran away. The temple
therefore takes its name from this rock, which can still be seen
next to the main hall. Eventually Sonmyo is said to have
transformed herself into a stone dragon, which now lies
beneath the main hall to protect the temple. Pusok-sa
subsequently became the leading temple of the Hwaom School.

Naksan-sa

Potalaka Temple

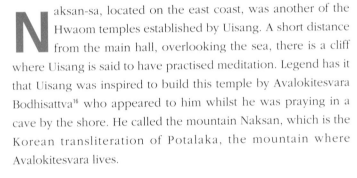

Naksan-sa, located on the east coast, was another of the Hwaom temples established by Uisang. A short distance from the main hall, overlooking the sea, there is a cliff where Uisang is said to have practised meditation. Legend has it that Uisang was inspired to build this temple by Avalokitesvara Bodhisattva[16] who appeared to him whilst he was praying in a cave by the shore. He called the mountain Naksan, which is the Korean transliteration of Potalaka, the mountain where Avalokitesvara lives.

Avalokitesvara appears in the Avatamsaka Sutra in the final chapter entitled "Gandavyuha" ("Entry into the Realm of Reality"). Here the pilgrim Sudhana travels to Mt. Potalaka to meet Avalokitesvara, who teaches Sudhana about his bodhisattva practice, which is to treat all beings with compassion and save them from suffering. His ultimate goal is to lead all sentient beings to the realm of reality or self-knowledge. Avalokitesvara also appears in the chapter of "Vast Teaching" in the Lotus Sutra[17].

Avalokitesvara has several names in Chinese. He/she is often referred to as the "Bodhisattva who hears the Sounds (or cries) of the World" or "the One with a Thousand Hands and a

Thousand Eyes". Actually, the original meaning of the word in Sanskrit is "looking into (contemplating) sound". So the practice being prescribed by Avalokitesvara is to contemplate sound and in so doing to trace the sense of hearing back to its origin, thereby attaining insight into the self-nature. This is one reason for the chanting of the familiar mantra "Kwanseum Bosal" in Korea. In Tibet, the equivalent mantra is the well-known "Om Mani Padme Hum".

At the popular level, the belief in Ava-lokitesvara as a deity with miraculous powers probably dates back to the 3rd Century AD. Around that time in China, the Bodhisattva took on a female appearance to become Guan-yin. In Korea, there are stories of miracles associated with belief in Kwanseum Bosal dating back as far as the Three Kingdoms period. Indeed, the chanting of "Kwanseum Bosal" remains the most popular and widespread form of Buddhist practice in Korea today.

Some time after Master Uisang had passed away, the temple was burned down. It was reconstructed in 858 AD by Zen Master Pomil (810-889), who was responsible for establishing the Sagul Mountain, Nine Mountains Zen School nearby at Kulsan-sa (see p.84). Today, Naksan-sa remains a popular pilgrimage site for prayer to Kwanseum Bosal.

Kuryong-sa

Nine Dragon Temple

Legend has it that Kuryong-sa was built on the site of a lake where nine dragons lived, which Master Uisang drove away with a magic formula. As the founder of the Hwaom School in Korea, Uisang had a profound influence on the development of Buddhism in the country.

Master Uisang lived simply in the true spirit of the Buddhist monk. He never possessed more than his simple robes and a bowl. When King Munmu (r.661-681) offered him lands and servants (which the larger temples of the time all possessed), he is reported to have declined by saying, "The Buddhist doctrine teaches equality. In it there is no distinction between high and low. The Mahaparinirvana Sutra says that we should not possess property unfairly gained. What use is land and what do I need servants for? The universe is my house and one bowl of food is enough for me. I live according to the teachings of the Buddha." [18] As a direct result of Uisang's efforts and exemplary life, the Hwaom doctrine derived from the Hwaom Sutra (which is the Korean name for the Avatamsaka Sutra) became a central pillar of Buddhism in Korea.

The Avatamsaka Sutra forms a part of the Mahayana texts and is supposed to be, along with the Mahaparinirvana Sutra of Com-

plete Enlightenment, the most advanced and highest teaching given by the Buddha. In the Avatamsaka Sutra, the speaker is Vairocana, the Resplendent Cosmic Buddha, who is expressing the perfect truth revealed in his enlightenment. The main doctrine teaches the theory of causation and that there is a universal and immutable mind that is the underlying reality of all phenomena. It teaches the complete and perfect mutual inter-penetration of all matter and the harmonious totality of all things in the perfectly enlightened Buddha mind.

The main theme of the Avatamsaka Sutra is the meaning of true enlightenment. It relates the travels of the young boy, Sudhana, in search of enlightenment. He is assisted by numerous spiritual friends along the way, all belonging to different walks of life, and eventually attains the truth with the guidance of Manjusri, the Buddha of Wisdom. In the end, the devotee makes a vow to follow the exemplary conduct of Samantabhadra, the Bodhisattva of selfless action.

Puryong-sa

The Temple of Buddha s Shadow

Puryong-sa takes its name from the shadow cast on the lake by the Buddha-shaped rock on top of the adjacent mountain. It was another of the temples established by Master Uisang. Today it is a Zen training center for nuns.

Master Uisang's Chart of the Avatamsaka Dharma-dhatu; The <Hwaom Bopkye Do> [19]

Since the Dharma nature is complete and inter-penetrating.
It is without any sign of duality.
All dharmas are unmoving and originally calm;
Without name or form, there are no distinctions.

The true nature is extremely profound, subtle and sublime.
It does not attach to self-nature but manifests according to causal
            conditions.
In one is all and in many is one;
One is identical to all and many are identical to one.

All the ten directions are contained in one particle of dust;
And so it is with all particles of dust.
Incalculably long eons are identical to a single thought instant;

A single thought instant is identical to incalculably long eons.

The moment that one begins to aspire with the heart,
Instantly perfect enlightenment is attained.
Illusion and reality become one,
And the particular and the universal merge without distinction.
This is the world of Bodhisattva Samantabhadra and the ten Buddhas.

In the Ocean Seal Samadhi of the awakened Buddha,
Many unimaginable miracles are produced according to one's wishes.
This shower of jewels benefiting all sentient beings fills the whole of
*   empty space;*
All sentient beings can receive this wealth according to their capacities.

Therefore, the one who practices contemplation returns to the primor-
*   dial realm,*
But without cutting off ignorance it can't be reached.
Through unconditional expedient means one attains complete freedom,
And so one returns home with riches.

By means of the inexhaustible treasure of the dharani,
Like jewels in a palace, one adorns the dharmadhatu.
Finally one returns and acts in the world;
That which is originally without motion is the Buddha.[20]

Pomo-sa

Heavenly Fish Temple

The name Pomo-sa comes from the legend of a golden fish that descended from heaven and lived in a well in a large rock at the top of the mountain. Pomo-sa, which became one of the ten great Hwaom temples, was founded by Uisang in the year 678 AD.

The founding of the temple was the result of a dream that King Munmu had during a period of Japanese attacks. It was reported that the Japanese were approaching Shilla with a large flotilla of ships and an army of 100,000 men. In his dream, a god appeared to him and told him to go to Kumjong ("Golden Well") Mountain with Master Uisang and recite the Hwaom Sutra for seven days and nights. If the recitation was completed and the country adopted the Hwaom teachings, the Japanese would be defeated and Korea would be safe from invasion. After the Japanese had been successfully repelled, Uisang was given a royal title and Pomo-sa was constructed on the slopes of the mountain.

The story shows how intimately Buddhism, as the adopted state religion, was bound up with the protection of the country. It also shows how quickly the Hwaom philosophy had spread throughout Shilla as a result of the writings of Wonhyo and the ceaseless teaching activities of Uisang.

The royal family actively supported the spread of Hwaom, which was adopted as the new philosophical and religious doctrine of the state. Perhaps coincidentally, the principle of harmonization laid the philosophical foundations for the political unification of the peninsula that occurred in 668 AD.

Bongjong-sa

Phoenix Pavilion Temple

It was long believed that this was another of the temples founded by Master Uisang. According to legend, Uisang selected this site for the temple after a paper phoenix, which he threw from nearby Pusok-sa, landed here at the foot of Ch'ondungsan Mountain. In 1972, during renovation work on the Kungnakch'on (the Masters' Hall), an inscription was found on one of the beams stating that the temple was founded by Uisang's disciple Nung'in Taedok. (The Kungnakch'on itself, which dates back to the early Koryo Dynasty (918-1392), is reputed to be the oldest extant wooden structure in Korea).

When Uisang passed away, he left behind ten accomplished disciples, of whom Nung'in Taedok was one. Each of these disciples formed their own teaching schools in different parts of the peninsula, and they became known as the Ten Mountains of Hwaom. Of these ten mountains, the main centers were at Pusok-sa (see p.46), Haein-sa (see p.62) and Hwaom-sa (see p.104). They were the driving force of Buddhism during the Shilla period and represented the cutting edge of philosophical thought at the time. Meanwhile however, a new and extremely vital force was already emerging in China that would shortly overturn all existing notions of what Buddhism was about.

Wolmyong-am

Bright Moon Hermitage

Wolmyong-am sits high up in the clouds at 450 meters, deep in Pyonsanbando National Park. This small hermitage is said to have been established in 691 AD by Pusol Kosa (layman) during the final phase of the Shilla kingdom. This date seems quite arbitrary however, since there are conflicting opinions as to when Pusol Kosa actually lived.

Pusol Kosa was the Layman Pang[21] of Korean Buddhism. Originally he was ordained as a monk. The story goes that he was traveling around the countryside various with two other monk companions, staying at temples and practising meditation. One night the three monks lodged at a country inn. Apparently the inn-keeper's daughter, Myohwa, fell madly in love with Pusol and wouldn't let him leave unless he married her, which Pusol finally consented to do.

Pusol lived by farming and fathered a son and a daughter with Myohwa. Meanwhile he continued to cultivate his practice and often visited the nearby temples, Naeso-sa and Kaeshim-sa. At some stage Pusol built Wolmyong-am, where he lived and practised with his family. This hermitage is named after his daughter. Later on he also built two further small hermitages, one for his son, called Tung'un-am, which is no longer extant, and the other, Myojok-am, for his wife Myohwa, who lived to the ripe old age of 110. It is said that the entire family was enlightened.

Wolmyong-am was burnt down and rebuilt on numerous occasions during its long history. Today there is a small Zen hall here.

Haein-sa

Ocean Seal Temple

Haein-sa, seated at the foot of Mt. Kaya, takes its name from the Buddha's "Ocean Seal" Samadhi, which is described in the Avatamsaka Sutra. In this state, the mind is likened to the surface of a perfectly calm sea in which the true image of all of existence is clearly reflected and everything is seen just as it is.

Haein-sa was one of the ten main mountain temples of the Avatamsaka School that was established by Master Uisang. It was founded in the year 802 AD by two enlightened monks, Master Sunung and his disciple, Ijong, who were both descendents of Uisang. According to legend, Master Sunung and Ijong, who had both just returned from China, were meditating in a small hermitage on the site of the present main hall when the wife of the Shilla king, Aejang, fell ill with an abscess on her back. As all medicines had proved useless, the king sent out officials to seek the help of revered monks. When the officials reached Mt. Kaya, they saw a mysterious radiance emanating from Sunung and Ijong, who were deep in samadhi. The officials asked the two monks to accompany them back to the palace in Kyongju, but they refused. Instead they gave the officials a spool of thread in five colours and told them to tie one end to the toe of the queen and the other end to a pear

tree in the courtyard of the palace. Their instructions were followed and the queen was cured whilst the pear tree dried up and died. The grateful king had a temple erected on the site of the hermitage and donated farmlands for the temple in the valley below.

A more credible story is given by Ch'oe Ch'iwon, a prominent writer and calligrapher who spent his final days in exile on Mt. Kaya. He wrote that the temple was erected in 802 AD by Sunung, who had attained enlightenment in China. The queen dowager was so pleased to hear the news that she converted to Buddhism herself and presented gifts and other means of support to the temple. Numerous students gathered to study here. After Sunung passed away, his disciple Ijong continued his work and completed the construction.

Since Haein-sa was founded in the 9th Century, many eminent Korean masters have in some way been associated with this temple, either training or teaching there. Today however, Haein-sa is probably most famous for being the temple where the Tripitika Koreana (The Complete Collection of Buddhist Scriptures in Eighty Thousand Blocks) is kept. The compilation of the Tripitika[22], as the Buddhist Canon is known, first took place during the reign of the Indian Emperor Asoka around 250 BC, some two centuries after the Buddha's death. The texts were copied by hand and translated into various languages over the following centuries as the Buddha's teaching spread throughout Asia. The first woodblock edition was created in 983 AD in China during the Sung Dynasty.

In 1087, the first Korean version was created in the hope of obtaining the Buddha's aid in repelling the Khitan invaders from the north. This first set was kept at Puin-sa temple near Taegu, but was destroyed by the Mongol invaders in 1232. The present version was carved between 1236 and 1251 at Sonwon-sa on Kanghwa Island and moved to Haein-sa in 1398 for safekeeping.

It is said that around thirty people were involved in the carving of the work and that each character was carved after performing a prostration to Buddha. Altogether there are 81,340 woodblocks divided into 6,791 volumes. The total number of characters is 52,382,960.

Today, Haein-sa symbolizes the Dharma (Buddhist teachings) and is one of the "Three Treasures" temples in Korea along with T'ongdo-sa and Songgwang-sa.

With each passing year people are becoming increasingly burdened with economic and other difficulties associated with modern life. What attitude do you think Buddhists should take in these changing times?

If you are a Buddhist and take refuge in the Buddha as your teacher, you shouldn't lose your center. You should try to control your desires and be satisfied with what you possess. We should lead our lives in this way. We should view the adversities generated by our karma as something that we can learn from.

Zen master Ta Hui of Sung dynasty China always taught: "Have few wants and be satisfied. Do not desire luxury. Endure hunger and thirst, and place your mind only on your practice." The world faces difficulties, as do temples. Monks have always lived in the spirit of simplicity possessing no more than a robe and bowl. So the Buddhist should not take these material difficulties too seriously. When we take the position of the student of life, everything exists as a teaching. People in the world should keep this attitude when they face difficulties. Do not be enticed by vanity and luxury. Do not hope for too much good fortune, be frugal and manage your household according to your earnings and position. Keep your lifestyle simple, and keep the attitude of the learner. That's the way to begin the new year.

Desires differ from person to person. Please say what kind of desires and vows Buddhists should cherish.

What is the meaning of a "Buddhist"? It means a disciple of the Buddha, the one who follows the teachings of Buddha. "Awaken and become a Buddha", that's the Buddha's message. After all, the first vow of the Buddhist is to "become a Buddha". However, becoming a Buddha alone is not enough. One should strive to help all living beings become Buddhas. This is the vow of the Bodhisattva which all Buddhists should strive to attain. Therefore, our vow for this year should be to think of our neighbours as ourselves.

Many merit making activities such as the founding of temples, the erecting of Buddhist statues and the publication and reciting of scriptures have been carried out over the last 10 years or so. So it is widely believed that now is the time when we shall see the appearance of many persons with superior spiritual capacities.

Merit making works produce no merit when they are done simply to gain merit for oneself. Then they are merely works of construction and nothing more. After all, Buddhist monasteries exist for the purpose of study. Of course, the construction of temples is necessary and good, but it should be carried out with sincerity and without the ulterior motive of gaining merit. Only in this way will one's own practice advance. Remember, a Buddhist temple is not a Buddhist temple when no practitioner resides there. So even if Buddhist pagodas are erected like wild geese in the sky and the eaves spread over the whole world, they still remain mere buildings if no sincere practitioners live and study there. A hundred years from now perhaps, the foundation and renovation of these temples will have proven their worth if one or two sincere Buddhists emerge from them.

What is much more important and meaningful than constructing temples however, is the preservation and spread of the Buddha's teachings through the exemplary conduct of Buddhists in their everyday lives. Buddhists should change their way of thinking. Merely constructing temples to gain personal merit has no meaning.

Every year during the retreat periods many aspirants devote themselves earnestly to their meditation practice in Zen halls. However it is said that amongst all these Zen practitioners today, there are no real Zen monks of great attainment, as there were previously.

When a fish stirs the water it becomes muddy. Consequently the other fish cannot be seen. Before one complains of the absence of people with true Zen understanding one should blame oneself for not possessing the insight to recognize such a person. If one has this insight then every living being is a Buddha. It was only the Fifth Patriarch Hung-jen who was able to recognize the Sixth Patriarch Hui-neng from among the five hundred students at Mt. Ts'ao Ch'i in China. By implication therefore, one's own discernment reflects one's own level of attainment. So when you are blind, nothing will be seen.

Every year around two-thousand Buddhists gather together for the summer and winter retreats. Still, it's said that true Zen practitioners are very few compared to the past. What do you think is the reason for this?

The future of Zen Buddhism lies in the very fact that every year two thousand or so people join meditation retreats with the intention of studying. That implies real earnestness. The monks who gather each season for the retreats have the earnestness to transcend birth and death. Without such earnestness nobody could endure a single retreat. It is amazing that every year we see an increase in the number of Zen practitioners entering into retreats. One cannot judge others as to whether they are real Zen practitioners or not. The true practitioner should always examine him/herself before evaluating the attainments of others. Only through keeping this spirit can the Buddhist tradition survive.

Can you give a word of encouragement to all those laypeople and monks who are endeavoring to practice Zen.

If you can hold your Hwadu properly, your life will not be disturbed. When you are really engaged in Hwadu practice, you won't be disturbed by the war raging all around you. That is real Zen practice. The practitioner should stop walking when he loses sight of the Hwadu, and should stop eating when the Hwadu becomes blocked. Ruminate on Lin-Chi's saying that in the midst of hunger and cold, awakening is not far off. So I ask you to keep practicing even in the face of adversity.

What is the most appropriate Hwadu/Kongan for our times?

People all too easily blame others whilst failing to reflect on their own shortcomings. Unless one reflects back on one's own mind, one's own failures will not become apparent. One's own behavior should always be carefully examined and one's own mind should always be cared for. Refrain from grasping and do not be disturbed by externals; in this way one will be able to see all situations objectively. So I suggest 'Naeshimmucho'on Woeshikcheyon' (do not grasp within and do not be moved from without) as an appropriate Hwadu for this year.

Laypersons are showing a lot of interest in Buddhism and are participating quite earnestly in Zen practice these days. What do you think of this trend?

In terms of practice there is no difference between becoming a monk and living in the world. Everyone is born and dies, and there is no exception to this regardless of whether one's head is shaved or not, whether one is a man or a woman, white or yellow-skinned. It is encouraging that laypersons are participating earnestly in Zen practice. An increasing number of Zen centers for lay followers have been established and more and more people have been joining them. This unusually high level of interest is really encouraging. Practicing while living in society is really desirable. To the real spiritual aspirant, wherever one lives is a temple, and every place one visits becomes a Zen hall; which means that one's whole life from morning to night becomes Zen practice.

What do you think of the current style of Zen practice, and particularly the Zen practice of 'Kanhwason' (Sudden Illumination Zen)?

'Kanhwason' is the most developed and direct way of Zen practice. Many aspirants attained insight through their practice of 'Kanhwason' and to date many Zen practitioners are still using this method.

The veracity of the Sudden Illumination tradition of Zen is supported by the numerous Kongan and teaching anecdotes found in the Mumonkan and the Blue Cliff Record. Blaming the method and teachings for your own lack of progress is akin to the bad workman who blames his tools. When you believe and trust in the correct teachings of the Patriarchs and in earnest take up your Hwadu, it can be guaranteed that there will be progress and ultimately realization.

Does the Dharmakaya, the realm of no birth and no death, really exist? If so, please tell me about it.

There is no special Dharmakaya as such. Seeing through the three poisons of desire, anger, and delusion; that is the Dharmakaya of no birth and no death.

Biography

Popjon Sunim was born in Hamp'yong, South Cholla province in 1925. He was ordained by Manam Sunim at Paegyang-sa in 1948, and recieved Inka from Songch'ol Sunim at P'agye-sa in 1951. After that, he practiced Zen at a number of temples and taught for fifteen years at the Zen hall of Sudo-am, Kimch'on, which he restored. Since 1985 he has been residing at Haein-sa, where he became Pangjang Sunim in 1966. Recently in March 2002 he was appointed as Chongjong (Head) of the Chogye order.

Songnam-sa

South Stone Temple

Zen Master Toui (d.825) is generally credited with being the founder of the Zen (K: Son) sect in Korea, as well as the founder of the Kaji Mountain School, one of the Nine Mountains Zen Schools. He was the first of several masters to bring the teachings of the great Chinese Zen Master Ma-tsu[23] (709-788) to Korea. He was born at a time when Buddhism in Shilla was beginning to lose its initial momentum and was becoming heavily institutionalized. In China, on the other hand, Buddhism was just entering into its golden age.

In the year 784 AD, Toui left for T'ang China, where he remained for thirty-four years. During his stay there, he studied under and received Dharma transmission from Zen Master Hsi-tang Chih-tsang[24] (735-814). His understanding was also recognized by Masters Pai-chang[25] (720-814) and Nan-ch'uan[26] (748-834). All of these masters were Dharma successors of the great Patriarch Ma-tsu (709-788). In 818 AD he returned to Shilla, bringing back with him the teachings of sudden enlightenment and the shock-tactic teaching style of the Ma-tsu school, which stressed an utterly non-intellectual approach and freedom from convention.

Unfortunately, the time when Toui returned to Korea was one of great social instability. It was a period of severe famines, peasant revolts and general lawlessness. Due to these very inhospitable circumstances, Toui was probably unable to do much to spread the Zen teachings. For the most part, Toui seems to have lived in semi-seclusion in the Sorak Mountains in the north of the country.

It is said that Songnam-sa was established by Master Toui in 824 AD, one year before he passed away, and that an octagonal stupa here contains his sarira. The temple itself, surrounded by imposing mountains with lofty peaks, has been renovated a number of times since then. Today it is a Zen training center for nuns.

Borim-sa

Precious Forest Temple ^{Kaji Mountain School}

At the time of Zen Master Toui's return to Shilla, the doctrinal Hwaom School, originally established by Uisang, had become the dominant form of Buddhism in Korea. It was not surprising therefore that when Toui began talking about sudden enlightenment, as opposed to academic study and cultivation, he met with resistance and indeed open hostility from the Buddhist establishment. After initially trying to introduce the Zen approach without much success, he retired to the Sorak Mountains, where he managed to pass on his lineage to Oksong Yomgo (d.844).

Oksong Yomgo in turn passed on the teaching to Pojo Ch'ejing (804-880), who later studied in T'ang China and achieved illumination after meeting many famous Zen masters. On his return to Shilla, with the assistance of King Hyonan (r. 857-861), Ch'ejing built Borim-sa temple on Mt. Kaji in 862 AD. Consequently this school, originally founded by Master Toui, became known as the Kaji Mountain School. Many people came to Borim-sa to study under National Master Ch'ejing, and when he passed away he is said to have had well over eight-hundred students. He did much to popularize Zen in the 9th Century.

In the <Sonmun Bojang Nok>, "The Records of the Zen

Family", compiled by Zen Master Chinjong Ch'onch'aek in 1293 (see p.140), there is an account of a conversation which Master Toui had with Master Chiwon, a contemporary Hwaom master:

Chiwon: "Is there any other Dharmadhatu (realm of reality) other than the four Dharmadhatus of Hwaom?"

Toui: "In Patriarchal Zen, one penetrates directly into the real aspect of the Dharmadhatu, and so the constriction of mere theory disappears like melting ice. So in Patriarchal Zen, no aspect of any Dharmadhatu can be found. There is no effort to be made for enlightenment nor any characteristics of wisdom. There is no chance for even Manjusri or Samantabhadra to appear in Patriarchal Zen."

Chiwon: "Is the so-called Patriarchal Zen (Zen of the Masters) a special teaching which cannot be found in the sutras?"

Toui: "In the teachings of Patriarchal Zen, there are no traces of either Buddhas or sentient beings to be found. There is only one's own true nature clearly revealed. That is why the teaching of Patriarchal Zen is outside of the sutras. The reason that the sutras try to explain about enlightenment through language is due to compassion for people of poor ability who are unable to grasp the meaning of Patriarchal Zen. Even though a person studies the sutras for a hundred years or more, if he cannot directly perceive his true nature, he'll never attain enlightenment."[27]

Songju-sa

Sages Abode Temple ^{Songju Mountain School}

Songju-sa was home to the Songju mountain school, another of the Nine Mountains Schools of Zen. Although the buildings have long since disappeared, judging from the remains of the site the temple complex must have been fairly extensive in its day. The temple was established by Master Muyom in 847 AD on the site of a previously existing smaller temple called Ohap-sa.

Zen Master Muyom (799-888) was of noble birth, an eighth-generation descendent of one of the kings of Shilla. During her pregnancy, his mother was said to have had various prophetic dreams about the destiny of her as-yet unborn son. When Muyom was twelve-years old he was ordained and was sent to Osaek Temple in the Sorak Mountains to study Buddhism. In 821 AD, he went to T'ang China and became the student of Master Ma-ku Po-che[28], one of the Dharma heirs of the Patriarch Ma-tsu. Master Ma-ku Po-che apparently foresaw that his Zen teachings would be carried eastward by a monk from Shilla, where they would flourish. Muyom remained in China for some twenty-four years, returning to Shilla in 845 AD. On his return, Muyom dedicated himself to spreading the "teaching of the direct mind-to-mind transmission of the Zen Patriarchs, which is not dependent on words or speech". He taught that the doctrinal teachings of the sutras can only be a partial and relative explanation of the truth whilst Zen, which is entirely non-conceptual, is the truth itself. He called the sutras "the land of language" and Zen "the land of no-language".

A student asked him, "What is the land of no-language?"
Muyom: "This is the land of Patriarchal Zen. In this world there is no master or disciple."
Student: "If that is the case, why is the relationship between master and disciple so important in Zen?"
Muyom: "Master Chang-ching said that the form of space is formless form and the function of space is causeless and spontaneous. Patriarchal Zen is like that also. Though a master transmits Dharma to the disciple, the transmission is a transmission without something transmitted. Therefore it is called a transmission which is no transmission."[29]

Like Pai-chang (749-814), whose dictum was "a day without work is a day without food", Muyom emphasised the importance of participating in daily chores. For him, drawing water and gathering firewood were the essence of Zen itself. This was the living statement of Ma-tsu's teaching that "everyday mind is the way". Muyom always wore the same clothes and ate the same food as the other monks, closely adhering to the simple and austere rules of the Zen school. He passed away at the age of ninety, leaving behind more than two hundred disciples.[30]

T'aean-sa

Temple of Great Peace ^{Tongni Mountain School}

T'aean-sa is one of the more remote Nine Mountains temples, located high on Mt. Tongni in the south-western part of Korea. Founded in 839 AD by Zen Master Hyech'ol (785-861), it is one of the two Nine Mountains temples that remain as active Zen training temples today.[31]

Hyech'ol was ordained at the age of fifteen at Pusok-sa, the main temple of the Hwaom sect. There he studied the Avatamsaka Sutra until 814 AD, when he left for China. In China, like Toui and Hongjik (see p.80), he studied under Master Hsi-tang Chih-tsang. Unfortunately for him however, Master Hsi-tang died in the same year that he arrived. Nevertheless, before Hsi-tang's death, Hyech'ol received transmission from the master, which indicates that he must have been an exceptional student. There is a story that indicates the intensity of his cultivation.

On his way from Shilla to China, Hyech'ol sailed on a ship that was carrying a number of convicts. When the ship arrived in T'ang, Hyech'ol was mistaken for a convict and put in jail. No one believed that he was a monk. Whilst in jail, Hyech'ol just quietly sat in samadhi, biding his time without complaining about his situation. He was condemned to die along with thirty other prisoners. When the time arrived for his execution, he was still sitting immersed in samadhi. Seeing his odd behaviour, his captors decided to make some further enquiries. Eventually they realized their mistake and he was released.

Returning to Shilla in 839 AD, he established T'aean-sa on Mt. Tongni, where hundreds of students came to study under him. He was also appointed a monk at the royal court by King Munsong (r.839-857) but he only stayed a short time before returning to the mountains. Hyech'ol was succeeded by Master Yunda (864-945), who led the Tongni Mountain School after his death. Zen Master Yunda was also highly respected in the royal court. One day King T'aejo asked him: "In the process of uniting the nation and bringing peace, I have killed many and tyrannized the country. How can I look after and protect the people from now on?" Yunda replied, "Your majesty, do not forget today's question, and the nation and the people will be at peace."[32] Hyech'ol's most famous student, however, was the monk Toson (827-898) (see p.100).

Shilsang-sa

Reality Temple ^{Shilsang Mountain School}

Shilsang-sa is set in a valley of verdant rice fields in the northern foothills of the majestic Chiri Mountains. The temple, which was once one of the foremost Zen training centers in the country, was established by Zen Master Hongjik, the founder of the Shilsang Mountain School of Zen, in the year 828 AD.

Not much is known about the life of Hongjik except that he went to T'ang China in 810 AD and, together with Toui and Hyech'ol, studied under the Chinese Zen Master Hsi-tang Chih-tsang. In the year 826 AD he received transmission from Master Hsi-tang and returned to Shilla. The remainder of his life he devoted to teaching at Shilsang-sa.

Ch'oe Koun, one of the most famous scholars in Shilla, wrote, "There was a Zen master named Hongjik. He studied Zen under Master Si-t'ang, attained enlightenment, returned home and resided on Mt. Namak. As for his Zen spirit, he practised without any trace of practice and attained enlightenment without any trace of enlightenment. In his daily meditation, he was always quiet like a great mountain and when he moved it was as though thunder was echoing around the mountains."[33] He is said to have had over one thousand disciples, of whom his successor Such'ol (d.893) was the most accomplished. It was Such'ol who turned Shilsang-sa into a large-scale Zen training center.

The temple complex was entirely reduced to ashes first during the Hideyoshi invasion of 1592, and then again during the reign of King Kojong (r.1864-1907). The temple was rebuilt on a much-reduced scale in 1884. The iron Buddha (in the picture) is believed to have been cast by Zen Master Hongjik himself in the 9th Century.

Bongnim-sa

Phoenix Forest Temple ^{Bongni Mountain School}

The origins of the Bongni Mountain School can be traced back to Zen Master Hyonuk (787-869). Hyonuk was ordained as a monk at the age of twenty-one and went to China in 824 AD. In China he studied under Master Chang-ch'ing Huai-hui[34] (755-815), another of the disciples of Zen Master Ma-tsu. He received Inka in 837 AD and returned to Shilla in the same year. After his return, Hyonuk is believed to have stayed and taught at Shilsang-sa in the Chiri Mountains, which means that Zen Master Hongjik had probably already passed away without leaving a fully trained successor. Master Hyonuk had more than five hundred disciples and was teacher to four of the kings of Shilla in succession, often being called upon to teach at the royal palace. It is said that at the end of the summer retreat of the year 869 AD, Hyonuk announced that he was going to depart from the world before the end of that year. Four months later he passed away.

Chingyong Shimhui (854-923) was the most prominent of Hyonuk's disciples. It was he who officially established the Bongni Mountain School in the year 897 AD at Bongnim-sa[35] on Mt. Bongni. Master Chingyong was born into the royal family, so he was able to establish Bongnim-sa under the patronage of the future king Hyogong (r.898-913). He had several hundred students.

Chingyong's disciple Ch'anyu Togwang (869-958) built up the Bongni Mountain School into the most prominent Zen school of the time. At the age of thirteen, Ch'anyu Togwang sought ordination from Priest Yungje, a student of Master Chingyong. According to the story, Yungch'e told him, "One day you will be a great dragon. At Bongnim Temple there is a real living Buddha. You should seek him out—his name is Chingyong Shimhui and he is a great master." Accordingly Ch'anyu, Togwang was ordained under Chinyong. In 892 AD, he went to China and studied under Master T'ou-tzu (?-914), receiving Inka from him. He returned to Korea almost thirty years later in 921 AD. Upon his return, he took up residence at Bongnim-sa and attracted thousands of believers to Zen Buddhism. He was highly regarded by King T'aejo (Wang Kon), the first king of the Koryo Dynasty, and the third king, Chongjong, made him "National Teacher".

Kulsan-sa

Steep Mountain Temple ^{Sagul Mountain School}

Kulsan-sa, the sixth of the Nine Mountains temples, was established by Zen Master Pomil in the year 851 AD. Pomil (810-889) was the son of the governor of Myongju Province. His father was apparently a compassionate man, and before Pomil was born his mother is said to have dreamt that she was holding the sun in her hands. Pomil was ordained at the age of fifteen, and in 831 AD he left for China to study Ch'an. In China Pomil became the student of Master Yen-kwan Chih-an (750-842), another of the numerous disciples of the great Patriarch Ma-tsu.

One day, Pomil asked Yen-kwan, "What is enlightenment?" The master replied, "The Tao (the way) cannot be attained by either cultivation or learning. You should not tarnish your mind with thoughts of either Buddha or enlightenment. If you constantly dwell in the one mind then that is Tao."[36] On hearing this, Pomil suddenly experienced a realization. He remained with Yen-kwan for six years.

Later he wandered throughout China and stayed at the monastery of Zen Master Yueh-shan[37] (745-828). When he first arrived, Master Yueh-shan asked him, "Where do you come from?" Pomil replied, "Kiangsi." "Why have you come?" asked

Yueh-shan. "To see you," said Pomil. "How did you get here?" asked Yueh-shan. "There's no way from there to here," replied Pomil, "but if you're going to take one more step up then I shan't be able to look into your face." "Wonderful! Wonderful!" exclaimed Yueh-shan, "The clear wind blowing from the outside makes a man's desire

cool. You have the true determination of the wandering monk to have come all the way here from so far away."[38]

After leaving Yueh-shan's temple, Pomil witnessed at first hand the Hui-cheng persecutions of Buddhism[39] (842-845) during which, by the Emperor's orders, over 4,600 large temples and monasteries and more than 40,000 smaller temples were destroyed. In 846 AD, after fifteen years in China, Pomil returned to Shilla and established the Sagul Mountain Zen School. For the remaining forty years of his life he stayed at Kulsan-sa, never leaving Mt. Sagul. One day in the spring of 889 AD he said to his students, "Shortly I'm leaving for the other world. I'm going now. Don't be sentimental. Just cultivate your minds and try not to sully the essential meaning of Buddhism."[40] The next day he passed away. Pomil left behind him a number of famous disciples including Nangwon Kaech'ong[41] (834-930) and Nanggong Haengjok[42] (833-918). Both Masters Nangwon Kaech'ong and Nanggong Haengjok were at different times appointed teacher at the royal court. Today nothing at all remains of Kulsan-sa.

Ssangbong-sa

Twin Peaks Temple

Ssangbong-sa, a small and unassuming rural temple, sits in a tranquil valley of rice paddies in the southwestern region of the peninsula. Technically it is not one of the original Nine Mountains temples, nor is it clear when it was established or by whom. It is believed, however, that this is the temple where Zen Master Ch'olgam Toyun (797-868), the founder of the Saja Mountain School, initially resided and taught upon his return from China in 847 AD. There is a stele here in his memory.

Toyun, who was from a noble family, was ordained as a monk at the age of eighteen. Initially he devoted his time to studying the Avatamsaka Sutra at one of the Hwaom temples established by Uisang. It seems, however, that he must have quickly become dissatisfied with this approach and undergone some kind of spiritual crisis, for he left the temple where he was staying and took to the life of the wandering beggar monk. In 825 AD he left for China, where he became the disciple of Master Nan-ch'uan P'u-yuan[43] (748-835), one of Ma-tsu's three closest students. Master Nan-chu'an was also the teacher of the famous Chao-chou[44] (778-897?). Toyun received Inka from Nan-chu'an in 847 AD and returned to Shilla in the same year.

After teaching for a number of years, on April 18th, 868 AD he gathered his disciples together. He said, "This physical body has a limited life. Now I'm leaving this world. You should maintain this temple and keep the light of the teachings shining brightly."[45] He then passed away. He was seventy-one years old, having been a monk for forty-four years. He passed on his lineage to his student Chinghyo.

Pophung-sa *Hungnyong-sa*

Flourishing Peace Temple ^{Saja Mountain School}

Hungnyong-sa on Mt. Saja is said to have been originally established by Master Chajang in the 7th Century. In the 9th Century, Zen Master Chinghyo Cholch'ung (826-900) greatly expanded the temple and developed it into one of the major Nine Mountains Zen training centers.

Chinghyo was ordained as a monk at the age of nineteen and trained under Master Toyun after his return from China. After his teacher's death, together with the monk Sog'un he moved Toyun's school here to Mt. Saja, from which the name of Toyun's school is derived. Chinghyo was greatly respected by the kings of the time, but staying true to the way of the simple Zen monk he declined to become teacher at the royal court. He died at Hungnyong-sa at the age of seventy-four while seated in the cross-legged meditation position.

Hungnyong-sa was burnt down in the 10th Century and from then on ceased to function as a Zen training center. Today it exists as a little-known and remote temple called Pophung-sa. The stele in the picture is dedicated to Zen Master Chinghyo and was erected in the 10th Century.

Bong'am-sa

Phoenix Cliff Temple ^{Huiyang Mountain School}

Bong'am-sa, sitting silently in a remote valley directly beneath Mt. Huiyang, is the largest Zen training center in Korea today. This Nine Mountains temple was established by Zen Master Tohon in 879 AD, somewhat later than the other Nine Mountains temples, yet the Huiyang Mountain School appears to predate the other schools by almost one hundred years.

According to the records of the Huiyang Mountain School, Zen Buddhism was first introduced from T'ang China to Shilla by Master Pomnang (d.646) during the reign of Queen Songdok (632-646). In China, Pomnang studied under Master Tao-hsin (580-651), the Fourth Patriarch of Zen Buddhism. Pomnang passed on his teachings to Shinhaeng (d.779) who also went to China and received transmission from Master P'u-chi (651-739), a disciple of Master Tao-hsin. Shinhaeng's successor was the monk Chunbom, who was succeeded by Hye-un. This implies that the origin of the Huiyang Mountain School predates the so-called Southern "sudden enlightenment" school of the Sixth Patriarch Hui-neng (638-713), from which all of the other Nine Mountains Schools trace their lineages.

Zen Master Tohon was born in Kyongju, the capital of Shilla, in 824 AD. When he was nine-years old he lost his father, and at the age of seventeen he was ordained as a monk at Pusok-sa Temple. Rather than going to China like most of his contemporaries however, Tohon trained under Zen Master Hye-un. Tohon was invited to become a monk at the royal court of King Hongang (r.875-886), but rather than accepting the position he established Bong'am-sa temple on Mt. Huiyang. In 882 AD he passed away in the sitting position at the age of fifty-nine and was posthumously honoured with the title Chijung Taesa (Great Master Wisdom Trace). He left behind a large number of disciples. His grand-disciple Chongjin Kyongyang (878-956), who studied in China for twenty-four years, became very famous and was patronized by King T'aejo, the founder of the Koryo Dynasty.

After the final Dharma meeting of the 1967 summer retreat at Kwanum-sa, the young Jinjae Sunim went before his teacher Zen master Hyanggok (1912-1978), to present his understanding. Jinjae began with a probing question to Hyanggok, who was seated before him.

"I'm not asking you about what Buddha realized; tell me something of the things that Buddha didn't realize."

"Nine times nine makes eighty-one."

"That's something that Buddha already knows!"

"Six times six makes thirty-six."

Jinjae asked again, "I'm not asking you about the eye of wisdom, but what kind of eye should the patch-robed monk possess?

"Only women can become Bhikkuni (nuns)."

In reply, Jinjae said, "Today, I've finally met a great master."

Zen master Hyanggok retorted, "Where have you seen him?"

"Katz!" exclaimed Jinjae Sunim.

"Correct, and correct again!" agreed Hyanggok Sunim.

The Dharma combat ended like that, and the Zen lamp, which had been passed down from Zen master Kyongho to Zen master Hyewol, to Zen master Unbong and then to Zen master Hyanggok, was transferred to Jinjae Sunim. Since that time, Jinjae Sunim has devoted himself to spreading the Zen teachings.

He founded Haeunjong-sa in Pusan in 1971 and was elected as the Chosil (Senior Zen master) of Kumdang Zen Center at Tonghwa-sa in 1994. On October 12, 2001, after thirty years of teaching, he was invited to become Chosil of the Taego Zen hall at Bong'am-sa. This interview took place at Haeunjong-sa on Nov. 27, 2001.

What are the special characteristics of Korean Zen?

> **The true spirit of Zen remains now only in Korea. The Zen tradition is today thread-like thin, but it still flows and is maintained in Korea.**

Then, it can be assumed that Korea must have many highly attained Zen monks? That does not seem to be the way that most people perceive the Korean Zen tradition though.

> **I am just a mountain monk, though I admit that monks who have opened the 'eye of wisdom' are rarely found. Unfortunately there is a shortage of real teachers who are able to guide monks in their practice. Also it seems that there are not enough truly devoted aspirants.**

Isn't the problem with 'Kanhwason' (Sudden Enlightenment Zen), the traditional style of Zen practice?

No, that is not correct. 'Kanhwason' is the correct way of Zen practice. Vipassanna or 'Mukchoson' (Silent Illumination Zen) may not necessarily lead practitioners to realization even after many lifetimes of practice. If however you truly take up the investigation of the Hwadu, you can be sure that finally you will be able to completely shatter and break through your worldly delusions. 'Kanhwason' can be practiced without words or letters and without going through any gradual stages of practice. Accordingly it is called the shortcut method and the direct gate (kyongjulmun) to enlightenment.

The Hwadus and Kongans which date back to T'ang and Sung Dynasty China seem to be still regarded as important and meaningful. Why can't we have new Hwadus and Kongans that reflect the situation and conditions of our times.

Each Kongan signifies or describes the ambit (kyonggye) of the particular realizations attained by prior Buddhas and Patriarchs of the Zen tradition. In the Hwadu we find the condensed teachings of the Buddhas and Patriarchs and the key to the mind to mind transmission of Zen. Does any distinction of past and present exist in the world of true realization? The ancient masters of China understood and attained the way of the Buddhas, so they offered the one thousand seven hundred Kongan as a way of communicating the same truth. So if we assiduously embrace and delve into these Kongan as they are, it is guaranteed that we will not be led astray.

It is said that in the past, Zen masters gave different Hwadus to each monk according to their individual dispositions, however I've heard that these days the same Hwadu is given to one and all.

It doesn't matter which Hwadu a monk is given if he has a deep faith. Whether one is given one of the Hwadu taken from the one thousand and seven hundred Kongan or whether a doubt or question spontaneously arises, it makes no difference. The important issue is whether the aspirant embraces the Hwadu wholeheartedly, and whether he pursues it with deep faith. It is not a question of this Hwadu or that Hwadu, and it does not depend on the teacher's teaching either. It depends on the aspirant's faith in the Hwadu and his way of pursuing the practice and study, not the question of which Hwadu he is given.

What if a doubt sensation is not stimulated when a Hwadu is given? After all the whole point of the Hwadu seems to be to stimulate doubt, no?

The Hwadu is not given so that it can be kept in the monk's bag or in the closet. The monk should be aware of why he shaved his head in the first place and should absorb himself solely in the Hwadu in order to achieve his goal. One should always offer the prayer: "may I attain great enlightenment for the salvation of all beings." Practice without this prayer is impossible. When a doubt is aroused, maintain the doubt so that great enlightenment may be attained. Offer the prayer in order to maintain the Hwadu like a flowing stream.

What was your Hwadu?

The first Hwadu I was given by my teacher Hyanggok Sunim was, "What is the meaning of Bodhidharma's coming from the West?" I broke through this Hwadu within two years, and could understand every Kongan except for "Sun faced Buddha; moon faced Buddha".

After a further five years of practice I was able to understand every Kongan.

"What is the meaning of Bodhidharma's coming from the West?" originates from the question that Master Chi Hsien of Hsiang Yen (? ~898) gave to people in order to teach them:

"A person is hanging from a branch by his mouth; his hands grasp no bough and his feet rest on no limb. Some passerby appears under the tree and asks him the reason that Bodhidharma came to China. If he answers, he'll fall and lose his life; if he doesn't answer, he fails to answer the question. So, what can he do in this case?"

To Chi Hsien's question, the leading monk Chao of Hu T'ou monastery replied: "I don't ask this question when the man is up the tree but before he climbs up. Will the Master say a word about that?" In response Chi Hsien roared with laugher. This Hwadu can be found in the Mumonkan, Case 5: "Man up a Tree".

"Sun faced Buddha; moon faced Buddha" is related to Ma-tsu of China (709~788). When the Great Master Ma-tsu was sick, his senior disciple visited him and asked, "How is your sickness these days?" Ma-tsu answered, "Sun Faced Buddha; Moon Faced Buddha". This case can be found in the Blue Cliff Record.

When one Hwadu is broken though, aren't all the other Hwadus also simultaneously broken through?

Many eminent Zen monks of the past attained two, three or even more realizations; but when you enter into the samadhi of 'one thought and no mind' and solve the Hwadu, your realization is complete there and then. However, in many cases a realization may suddenly come without entering into this state. Such a realization though is a minor one, due to one's partial or one-sided entrance into the truth. This is the reason for having two or three successive realizations. However, when one attains realization in the samadhi of 'one thought and no mind', it is complete and thoroughgoing; then there is no more to be realized.

Is there any difference for monks and laypersons in the process of breaking through the Hwadu?

One must give up one's very life in order to penetrate the Hwadu. The Hwadu is broken through when other thoughts are removed. But if one stays in the world that is very difficult. Breaking through the Hwadu occurs when one is able to maintain one thought.

What is your wish, if you have one?

My wish is to meet another with the same understanding as myself.

Jinjae Sunim was entirely spontaneous throughout our conversation. He was like a skilled swordsman in a duel. He pointed out that Zen monks who cannot give direct answers in 'Dharma combat' cannot have attained the way. They are no different to swordsmen who will be killed because of their hesitation in blocking their enemy's thrusts. His maxim is 'salbulsaljo', which means, "Should a Buddha appear strike him down, should a Patriarch appear strike him down". After the interview was finished, as I was walking out of Haeunjong-sa, I noticed the big sword of a Zen monk hanging over the gate of deliverance (Haet'almun).

Biography

Jinjae Sunim was born in Namhae, South Kyongsang province in 1934. He was ordained by Sogu Sunim in 1954, and received Inka from Zen master Hyanggok in 1967. He founded Haeunjong-sa in Pusan in 1971, and was selected as Chosil (Senior Zen master) of Kumdang Zen Center at Tonghwa-sa in 1994. Currently he is Chosil of Taego Zen Center at Bong'am-sa, which was recently designated as a special Zen center belonging to the Chogye order.

Wolgwang-sa

Moonlight Temple

In addition to the Nine Mountains Schools of the late Shilla period, there was another Zen school, which for reasons not clearly understood was never included among them. This was the Wolam Mountain School established by Master Wollang. Wollang, like many of his contemporaries, studied in China and received transmission from Zen Master Cheng-chu. In the year 864 AD he returned to Shilla and established a training center here at Wolgwang-sa on Worak Mountain.

The last of the Nine Mountains Schools to be established was the Sumi Mountain School, founded by Master Iom (870-936). Iom was born in Kyongju, the Shilla capital, and ordained as a monk at the age of sixteen. In 896 AD, he joined the party of a T'ang envoy and travelled to China to study Ch'an. He studied under Master Yun-chu Tao-ying, the disciple of Master Tung-shan Liang-chieh[46] (807-869), the founder of the Ts'ao-tung (J: Soto) line.

When Iom arrived at his temple, Master Yun-chu asked him, "Since we didn't part so long ago, why do we meet again so soon?" Iom replied, "What do you mean, meet again? We've never been parted!" Iom stayed with Yun-chu for some six years and eventually received Inka from him. On departing,

Yun-chu said, "The spirit of my teacher Tung-shan is now going to the eastern land."[47]

Iom returned to Shilla in 911 AD and became a monk at the royal court at the invitation of King T'aejo, the founder of the Koryo Dynasty. In 932 AD, T'aejo built Kwangjo-sa[48] for him on Mt. Sumi, and thereafter Iom's line became known as the Sumi Mountain School. Hundreds of students gathered at this temple to study under Iom. Four years later Iom passed away at the age of sixty-seven at Oryong Temple in the capital, Kaesong.

Ch'ong'am-sa

Clear Rock Temple

Ch'ong'am-sa, situated in a remote valley beneath Mt. Puryong, was first established as a small hermitage in the year 858 AD. It was reputedly built by the famous monk Toson (827-898), who lived at the beginning of the Koryo Dynasty.

Master Toson was one of the most influential monks of the 9th Century. He studied under Master Hyech'ol at T'aean-sa and became one of his successors. Apart from his activities as a Zen master, he is mainly known for his use of esoteric Tantric Buddhist practices and for importing the techniques of geomancy (Feng-shui) from China.

In China, Toson studied the ideas of the Esoteric Buddhist Master I-Hsing (673-727), who was the most famous of the T'ang astronomers and mathematicians. I-Hsing was responsible for combining the traditional Chinese ideas of divination based on the cosmology of the I Ching and the theory of Feng-shui with Buddhist philosophy. In this way he developed new ideas in Esoteric Buddhism based on geomancy and cosmic forces.[49]

When Master Toson returned to Korea, he introduced these concepts as a way to both develop the nation and to popularize

Zen Buddhism. Through his efforts, the theory of Feng-shui later became an integral part of Korean culture. According to Toson, these esoteric sciences were "the Dharma by which the great Bodhisattvas save the world". Most likely, however, people were still not ready to accept the very direct teachings of Zen and he was using skilful means to convince them.

According to legend, he put 3,800 marks on a map of the Korean Peninsula and said, "Just as a person is cured by applying acupuncture and cauterized using moxa, so too the nation. When mountains and rivers are sick, the disease can be cured by building temples, Buddha statues and stupas in particular places."[50]

Ch'ong'am-sa itself was completely destroyed by fire on two occasions, first in 1647 and then again in 1782, after which it was not reconstructed again until 1897. Unfortunately, the main hall burnt down yet again in 1911 and had to be rebuilt the next year. In 1987 Ch'ong'am-sa became a training temple for nuns.

Toson-sa

Way Gathering Temple

Toson's ideas were expressed in his writings, the "Records of Master Toson" <Toson Shilgi> and the "Esoteric Teaching of Zen Master I-Hsing" <Ilhaeng Sonsa Bongbal Lok>. He taught that although the mountains and rivers of the country are in essence beautiful, there are many deep valleys in which lurk thieves as well as other misfortunes such as droughts and floods. He advised that to protect the nation from these and other disasters, temples, stupas and Buddha statues should be built throughout the country: the temples would support the sick parts of the earth, the stupas would curb the energies in geomantically unfavourable places, and vulnerable places would be protected from thieves by the stone Buddhas.[51]

General Wang Kon, who founded the Koryo Dynasty (937-1392) and became King T'aejo (r.918-943), was greatly influenced by Toson's ideas on protecting the nation. Toson helped in the selection of the site for the capital of the new dynasty and also became the king's personal advisor and National Teacher. Following Toson's ideas, T'aejo was responsible for the construction of over 3,800 new temples during his reign. Nevertheless, although Toson himself advocated this policy, he insisted, "the merit and virtue of building temples and stupas is not better than learning the deep

reasoning of Zen."[52]

Toson-sa, perched high up on Mt. Tobong, was another of the temples established by Toson who, during his travels around the country, was deeply moved by the scenic beauty of this site. The temple, which was initially just a small hermitage, was built in 862 AD. While staying here Toson is said to have foreseen that about one thousand years in the future Buddhism would start to decline, and eventually fade away. He believed, however, that it would be revived again at some future time. After this revelation he used supernatural powers to sculpt from rock a seven-meter tall statue of the Bodhisattva Avalokitesvara, which can still be seen at Toson-sa today.

Hwaom-sa

Flower Garland Temple

Hwaom-sa, located on the southern slopes of the Chiri Mountains, is one of the most sublime of all the Korean Buddhist temples. It is named after the Hwaom Sutra (Skt. Avatamsaka Sutra), which teaches the universal oneness of all things. Hwaom-sa therefore, like Haein-sa and the other Hwaom temples, is dedicated to Vairocana, the universal cosmic Buddha of the Avatamsaka Sutra. The temple was first established by the enlightened Master Yongi in 554 AD and was expanded by Master Uisang in 634 AD when it became one of the so-called Ten Mountains of Hwaom. By the 10th Century it had become one of the two leading centers of the Hwaom school in the country (the other being Haein-sa).

At the end of the Shilla period, the Hwaom school, which had been established by Uisang and centered around Pusok-sa (see p.46), had become divided. The so-called "South Mountain" School led by Master Kwanhye (?-936) was centered here at Hwaom-sa, whilst the "North Mountain" School was led by Master Huirang at Haein-sa (see p.62). Essentially, the "North Mountain" School followed the approach of Uisang whilst the "South Mountain" School followed the approach of Fa-tsang, the third patriarch of Hwaom in China.

The difference between the two approaches was that Fa-tsang's method was more analytical and deconstructivist. Through his extremely detailed commentaries on the Avatamsaka Sutra, he emphasized the necessity of understanding each element or aspect of reality separately as the way to grasp the whole. In Master Uisang's point of view on the other hand, insight into the totality could be attained through the penetration of just one single aspect of the Dharmadhatu. Despite the different approaches of Master Huirang and Master Kwanhye, these two masters did much to develop the study of Hwaom during this period.

Hwaom-sa was destroyed during the Hideyoshi invasions of the late 16th Century but was rebuilt by Master Pyogam (see p.200) in 1630. Prior to the invasions, the entire Avatamsaka Sutra had been carved on stone blocks at this temple, but during the invasions they were completely smashed. Today the pieces are enshrined in the main hall.

Chijok-am

Hermitage of the Tusita Heaven

Chijok-am is one of the sixteen hermitages belonging to Haein-sa on Mt. Kaya. It is not known exactly when this hermitage was first built, but originally it was called Tosol-am, the Hermitage of Tusita (one of the Buddhist heavens). It is situated next to Huirang-dae (the Hermitage of Master Huirang), where Avatamsaka Master Huirang (815-886) lived and attained enlightenment. He also used to chant and meditate here at Chijok-am.

Master Huirang was a contemporary of Master Toson (see p.100), and like Toson, he was very much respected by King T'aejo (r. 918-943), the founder of the Koryo Dynasty (918-1392). Master Huirang was quite exceptional, and there are many miracles associated with his life. There is even a legend that when King T'aejo was fighting against Prince Wolgwang, Huirang sent divine soldiers to the king to lead him to victory.

At the Haein-sa Museum there is a statue which Huirang made of himself. There is a hole in the area of the heart. It is said that Master Huirang came from the place where all beings have holes in their hearts.

Kap-sa

Armour Temple

According to the "Memorabilia of the Three Kingdoms", Kap-sa, located high on the slopes of the mystic Mt. Kyeryong, was originally founded in the year 420 AD during the reign of King Kuishin of Paekche. The main halls were reconstructed by a certain Master Hye-myong in the year 556 AD. Subsequently, the temple became one of the ten centers of the Hwaom School set up by Master Uisang.

By the 10th Century however, in the face of the growing strength and popularity of the Zen school, as well as increasing doctrinal disputes within, the Hwaom School was beginning to splinter. At this time Master Kyunyo (923-973) assumed the responsibility of trying to reconcile the two different viewpoints of Fa-tsang's South Mountain and Uisang's North Mountain schools. Although he himself was from the South Mountain branch of the Hwaom School, his writings were devoted to creating a synthesis of the two. From his point of view, it was unnecessary to distinguish between the two approaches since reality in itself is complete and therefore capable of embracing both approaches. Kyunyo called his system "Chuch'uk", meaning "throughout, from each and every side". Altogether, Kyunyo wrote some sixty-nine books expounding his ideas, eighteen of which were originally kept here at Kap-sa.

As well as travelling extensively around the country trying to unite the Buddhist community, he also tried to bring harmony to society at large. He wrote a number of simple and amusing verses in order to educate the ordinary people about the ideas of Hwaom. These were put to music and enjoyed considerable popularity. Furthermore, Kyunyo himself was credited with having supernatural powers which he used to help people according to the necessity of the situation. Because of this he was greatly admired by King Kwangjong, who often sought his advice.

The temple was completely burnt down during the Hideyoshi invasions of the late 16th Century and rebuilt in 1604. During the Choson Period the name was changed from Kye-ryong Kap-sa to Kap-sa. Today there is a small Zen hall above the main temple. Interestingly, there is a pagoda here built over the burial site of an ox that died of exhaustion while carrying the construction materials for the original temple in the year 419 AD.

Sonam-sa

Hermit Rock Temple

According to one source, this temple was founded in 542 AD by the monk Ado and was called Piro-am. According to another, the temple was established by Toson in 875 AD and was called Sonam-sa. The name Sonam-sa derives from the large and flat rock on which two hermits used to play Paduk (Korean Chess). In 1088 the temple was renovated by Master Uich'on (1055-1101), who lived here after he returned from China.

Uich'on, who was the fourth son of King Munjong (r.1046-1083), was one of the major figures of Buddhism during the Koryo Dynasty. In 1085, at the age of thirty, he secretly travelled to Sung China and studied under famous teachers of the Tien-tai[53], Hua-yen[54] and Ch'an[55] schools. Upon his return, his main goal was to try to reconcile the differences between the Zen school and the doctrinal Hwaom school, which had become almost completely alienated from each other. The Zen school had reached the point where any kind of scriptural study was completely shunned, whilst the doctrinal school had become almost totally involved in theoretical disputation. Uich'on considered that both schools were losing touch with the essential teachings of Buddhism. To this end he revived the Ch'ont'ae school, founding the temple Kukch'ong-sa in 1097

with the support of his mother Queen Inye. The Ch'ont'ae School was the counterpart of the Tien-tai School of China, the teachings of which are based on the Lotus Sutra. From this point of view, the study of Buddhist texts and the pursuit of meditation are complementary and should go hand in hand.

Master Uich'on was a formidable scholar and it was he who rediscovered and realized the great value of Wonhyo's achievements (see p.40). Uich'on credited the origins of the syncretic Ch'ont'ae School to Master Wonhyo, and was responsible for the revival of interest in Wonhyo's writings. Uich'on also brought back with him some 1,010 Buddhist commentaries from China and had them carved on wooden blocks. These became known as the Supplement to the Tripitika. Unfortunately Uich'on died at the early age of forty-six before he could see his work completed, and the Supplement itself didn't last long either--it was destroyed together with the entire Tripitika during the Mongol invasion in 1231.

The old temple sits peacefully amidst blue mountains.

My brushwood gate opens and closes to the clouds.

A bottle for water and an old staff are my only possessions:

Who cares about the passing of the years.[56]

Uich'on

Kojo-am

The Patriarch s Hermitage

Kojo-am was built during the reign of King Kyongdok (r.742-764) as an independent temple much earlier than Unhae-sa, the main temple to which it now belongs. It is not clear when it became affiliated with Unhae-sa, but it was here that Master Chinul first established his famed Meditation and Wisdom Community during the 12th Century. Today the hermitage is a very popular place for prayer and many miracles are associated with the site.

Pojo National Master Chinul (1158-1210) is undoubtedly the seminal figure associated with Zen Buddhism in Korea. He is arguably the only truly original Buddhist thinker to have been born on Korean soil and his teachings and writings have had a more far-reaching impact than those of any other Korean Zen master. Ironically, his attainment came entirely through his own efforts and he never went to China to study. Perhaps for this reason, his understanding of Zen is firmly rooted in the Buddhist scriptures themselves. It is probably this fact that enabled him to completely transcend the long-standing divide between the Zen and the Doctrinal Schools.

Master Chinul was born into an aristocratic family, but as a child his health was poor. His father prayed to Buddha that if

his son became well, he would send him to be ordained as a monk. Chinul's health improved and accordingly he was ordained at the age of seven. At fifteen he received the precepts at Kulsansa, one of the Nine Mountains Zen Schools (see p.84). In 1182 at the age of twenty-four he passed the royal examinations for Zen monks held each year in the capital. However, disgusted by the pursuit of power, wealth and fame that had become the goal of many Buddhist monks, he vowed along with nine other monks to establish a retreat community dedicated to the pursuit of wisdom and meditation. After this he left the capital.

In 1184, Chinul attained his first awakening while reading a passage from the Platform Sutra of the Sixth Patriarch, which says, "The self-nature of suchness gives rise to thoughts. But even though the sixth sense faculties see, hear, sense and know, it is not tainted by the myriad of images. The self-nature is constantly free and self reliant."

According to his memorial stele, after reading this, "Astonished, he was overjoyed at gaining what he had never experienced before, and getting up, he walked around the hall, reflecting on the passage while continuing to recite it. His heart was satisfied. From that time on, his mind was averse to fame and profit; he desired only to dwell in seclusion in mountain ravines. Bearing hardship joyfully, he aspired to the path; he was obsessed with this quest."[57] It was this experience which no doubt laid the

foundation of the main tenet of his teachings, that of "Sudden enlightenment followed by gradual cultivation." He had realized that the true nature could never be gained by practice, since it was not something that had ever been apart from him in the first place.

His second realization came in 1185. As he himself later wrote, "I came upon the simile about 'one dust particle containing thousands of volumes of sutras in the Avatamsaka Sutra.' The passage went on to say, 'The wisdom of the Tathagatas is just like this: it's complete in the bodies of all sentient beings. It is merely that ordinarily people are not aware of it and do not recognize it.' I put the sutra volume on my head (in reverence) and unwittingly started to weep."[58] This confirmed in his mind that there was no contradiction between the transmission of Zen and the writings contained in the sutras.

Then, some eight years after he had originally vowed to establish a meditation community with his fellow monks, he received an invitation from one of the remaining members of this group to establish such a community at Kojo-am. In 1190 the Samadhi and Prajna community was formally established at this temple and the first retreat began. It was open not only to monks but also to any layperson who was dedicated to the practice of meditation.

Songgwang-sa

Temple of the Vast Pines

By 1197, a large number of practitioners had joined the Meditation and Wisdom Community. As Chinul was the most experienced, he came to assume more and more the role of teacher in this community. However, it soon became apparent that Kojo-sa had become too small.

At the beginning of the year, Chinul found the remains of a temple called Kilsang-sa on Mt. Songgwang. The temple was not large, but he wrote that "The site was outstanding and the land was fertile; the springs were sweet and the forests abundant. It was truly a place which would be appropriate for cultivating the mind."[59]

In the spring of 1197, Chinul moved the Meditation and Wisdom Community to this new site, and work began on the reconstruction and expansion of the existing temple. This work took nine years and was not completed until 1205. To mark the occasion, King Huijong (r.1204-1211), who much admired Chinul, issued a proclamation calling for 120 days of celebration. The name of the temple was changed to Suson-sa and the name of the mountain was changed to Mt. Chogye, after the mountain in China where Hui-neng, the Sixth Patriarch, had his temple. (It was several centuries later that the temple's name was changed to Songgwang-sa).[60]

Meanwhile, between 1197 and 1200 Chinul and a number of the members of the community entered into an intensive retreat at Sangmuju-am, a remote hermitage in the nearby Chiri Mountains. It was here that Chinul had his third and decisive awakening. As he himself recorded,

"I went to live on Mt. Chiri and found a passage in the Records of the Zen Master Ta-hui P'u-chueh, which said: 'Zen does not consist in quietude; it does not consist in bustle. It does not involve logical discrimination. Nevertheless, it is of utmost importance not to investigate Zen while rejecting quietude or bustle, the activities of daily life or logical discrimination. If your eyes suddenly open, then Zen is something which exists inside your very own home.' I understood this passage. Naturally, nothing blocked my chest again

and I never again dwelt with the enemy. From then on I was at peace.[6]

These three enlightenment experiences formed the philosophical basis of his teaching.

In teaching students, Chinul formed a system of three approaches, or gates, which came to be known collectively as "Pojo Zen". The first of these was the cultivation of meditation and wisdom. This was the practice of "holding oneself in the equanimity of clearness and calmness", and could be described as the balanced development of samadhi and prajna in equal proportion. In this state, a person is aware of everything, just seeing things as they are without discrimination. Chinul explained this in his Secrets of Cultivating the Mind:

"Samadhi is the essence; prajna is the function. Since prajna is the functioning of the essence, it is not separate from samadhi. Since samadhi is the essence of the function, it is not separate from prajna. Since in samadhi there is prajna, samadhi is calm yet constantly aware. Since in prajna there is samadhi, prajna is aware yet constantly calm."[62]

Related to this was his concept of "sudden enlightenment followed by gradual practice"[63], which he explained as follows:

"First let us take sudden awakening: When the ordinary man is deluded, he assumes that the four great elements are his body and the false thoughts are his mind. He does not know that his own nature is the true Dharma body; he does not know that his own numinous awareness is the true Buddha. He looks for the Buddha outside of his own mind. While he is thus wandering aimlessly, the entrance to the way might by chance be pointed out by a wise advisor. If in one thought he then follows back the light (of his mind to its source) and sees his original nature, he will discover that the ground of this nature is innately free of defilement, and that he himself is already endowed with the non-outflow wisdom nature which is not a hair's breadth different from that of all the Buddhas. Therefore it is called sudden awakening."

"Next let us consider gradual cultivation. Although he has awakened to the fact that his original nature is no different from that of the Buddhas, the beginningless habit-energies are extremely difficult to remove suddenly, and so he must continue to cultivate while relying on his awakening. Through this gradual permeation,

his endeavours eventually reach completion. Hence it is called gradual cultivation.[64]

The second gate of "Pojo Zen" was faith and understanding. The crucial point that he emphasized was that awakening does not consist of gaining something new but rather in realizing that one is already a Buddha. This approach was based on Chinul's thorough philosophical understanding of the Avatamsaka Sutra.[65]

The third approach that Chinul advocated was the shortcut of investigating the "Hwadu"[66]. The Hwadu method was developed by the Chinese Sung Dynasty master, Ta-hui[67] (1089-1163) to negate the overly conceptual and intellectual approach that was starting to take root in the Chinese Zen establishment of the 11th and 12th Centuries. Master Ta-hui was a 17th-generation successor of Lin-chi I-hsuan (d.867, K: Imje, J: Rinzai) and it was he who was largely responsible for re-invigorating the Chinese Zen school in the 12th Century. He explains the Hwadu method[68] as follows:

"A monk once asked Chao-chou, 'Does a dog have Buddha nature?' Chao-chou said, 'Mu!'[69] This one character 'Mu', is the stick by which all false images and ideas are destroyed at their very foundations. To it you should add no judgements about being or non-being, no arguments, no bodily gestures like raising your eyebrows or blinking your eyes. Words have no place here. Neither should you throw this 'Mu' character away into the nothingness of emptiness, or seek it in the comings and goings of the mind, or try to trace its origins in the scriptures. You must only continuously raise this (Hwadu) around the clock. Sitting or lying, walking or standing, you must give yourself over to it completely. 'Does a dog have Buddha nature?' The answer: 'Mu' Without withdrawing from

everyday life just continuously look into this Hwadu!

"You must concentrate yourself into this 'Mu', with all your 360 bones and your 84,000 pores, making your whole body one great mass of inquiry. Work on it intently day and night. Do not attempt nihilistic or dualistic interpretations. It is like having swallowed a red hot iron ball. You try to vomit it out, but you cannot... When you begin to find it entirely devoid of flavour, that means that the final moment is approaching. Do not let it slip out of your grasp. When all of a sudden something flashes out in your mind, its light will illuminate the entire universe and you will see the spiritual land of the Enlightened One fully revealed at the point of a single hair, and the great wheel of the Dharma revolving in a single speck

of dust."⁷⁰

Chinul was the first Korean master to adopt Ta-hui's Hwadu approach. It is quite possible that whilst living in the southern region of the peninsula, near the coastal ports, he was able to directly receive various copies of Ta-hui's writings from China. The Hwadu method that Chinul adopted subsequently became the primary tool used for teaching Zen in the Korean tradition. Today it remains the main method used in Zen halls throughout the country.

Looking at the three approaches of Chinul, the first can be understood as the basic principle of practice. The second is the foundation upon which the practice rests. And the third is the method of sustaining the practice. What made Chinul's system so meaningful in the 12th Century was that he managed to synthesize the practice of Zen with the teachings of the sutras.

"On the morning of April 22nd, 1210, Chinul asked his attendant, 'What day is it today?' When told the day, the Master donned the ceremonial Dharma robe and then ordered the monastery drum to be beaten to summon the monks of the community. Carrying his staff with six rings, he walked over to the Dharma hall where he lit incense and ascended the platform. Then he struck his staff and said, 'The miraculous efficaciousness of the Zen Dharma is inconceivable. Today I have come here because I want to explain it fully to all of you in the assembly.' He proceeded to answer the different questions put to him. Finally a monk asked, 'I'm not sure whether the past illness of Vimalakirti of Vaishali and today's sickness of the Master are the same or different?' The Master replied, 'You're only learned similarity and difference!' Then, he picked up his staff and struck it several times and said, 'A thousand things and ten thousand objects are all right here.' Finally, supported by his staff, he remained completely immobile and passed away."[13]

It was reported that seven days after his death his complexion was the same as when he was still alive and his hair and beard continued to grow as usual. When his body was cremated, the bones radiated five colours, and thirty large sarira were collected. The king conferred upon him the posthumous title of "National Master Puril Pojo" (Buddha-Sun Shining Universality).

Questioner: "You say that the Buddha-nature exists in the body right now, so then if it's present in the body right now, ordinary people too must possess it. If this is the case then why can't we see it?"

Chinul: "It is in your body, but you do not see it. Ultimately, what is that thing which during the twelve periods of the day knows hunger and thirst, cold and heat, anger and joy? This physical body is a synthesis of the four elements: earth, water, fire and wind. Since matter is passive and insentient, how can it see, hear, sense and know? That which is able to see, hear, sense and know is your Buddha nature. For this reason, Lin-chi said: 'The four great elements do not know how to expound dharma or listen to dharma. It is only that formless thing in front of your eyes, clear and bright of itself, which knows how to expound dharma or listen to dharma.' This 'formless thing' is the dharma-seal of all the Buddhas: it is your original mind. Since this Buddha-nature exists in your body right now, why do you ignore it and vainly seek satisfaction elsewhere?"[72]

From "Chinul's Secrets on Cultivating the Mind", written by Chinul between 1203 and 1205.

*D*ay for the Zen monk starts early, well before the dawn, with the sound of Avalokitesvara's 'Chant of the One Thousand Hands and Eyes', accompanied by the rhythmic 'tok, tok, tok' of the mokt'ak, which suddenly breaks the still silence of the night. Like the chugging of a distant locomotive, this slow but insistent sound comes drifting in through the rice-paper thin doors of the meditation hall at around 3 am, to bring the Zen monks gently back to waking consciousness. As the chanting monk makes his way around the monastery, the 'tok, tok, tok' intermittently fades and becomes more insistent, while the half-asleep Zen monks' minds drift back and forth between this world and the worlds of their dreams. Gradually, the monks in the Zen hall rise, fold their bedding and go outside to wash their faces. Three sharp claps of the chukpi (the bamboo clapper), three bows to the Buddha and another day of sitting meditation begins.

The meditation hall is simple and sparse. The meditating monks, with their shaved heads and grey robes, sit back to back in the cross-legged position in two neat rows facing outward towards the white-papered walls of the meditation hall. Each monk sits on a brown cushion, which also doubles as his sleeping mat, placed directly on the floor. (This is in contrast to the Japanese and Chinese traditions where the monks generally sit on an elevated platform.) The yellow oiled rice paper floor is 'ondol', which means that it is heated during the long cold winter months. At one end of the hall there is a long bamboo rod suspended along the wall along which hang the brown ceremonial 'kasa' of the monks. Above this there is a narrow wooden shelf on top of which are placed the monks' bowls. At the other end of the hall there is a wall-clock, but other than that there is nothing to distract the Zen monks from their objective of transcending birth and death.

As soon as the chukpi is struck three times by the head monk, the monks assume the cross-legged meditation posture and start to focus their minds on their 'Hwadu'. Usually after a few deep breaths the mind starts to settle down and concentration on the Hwadu becomes possible. Eyes open (to prevent drowsiness) the monks let their gaze gently fall on the floor 2-3 feet in front of where they sit. As distracted thoughts become fewer, concentration slowly becomes deeper. Fifty minutes later the chukpi is again struck by the head monk. The meditators rise from their cushions and start to walk fairly briskly around the Zen hall in single file following the head monk. This brisk walking relieves cramped legs and stimulates the blood circulation, which in turn prevents drowsiness. After 10 minutes of walking, the monks return to their cushions and resume the cross-legged posture. The chukpi is struck once, and the next 50-minute meditation period begins. With the exception of meals and rest periods, this procedure continues throughout the day.

At 10:30 there is a brief rice offering ceremony to the Buddha lasting no longer than 15 minutes, which takes place in the main shrine hall of the monastery. The monks don their ceremonial 'kasa' and then in single file walk over from the Zen Hall to the Shrine Hall. The monks chant the 'Three Refuges' followed by the 'Heart Sutra'. Then three quick bows and the monks walk in single file back to the Zen Hall where they take lunch.

Meals are taken three times a day in the Zen hall. They are a quick

and ordered affair; and are virtually identical. Each monk sits with his four wooden bowls in front of him, into which go rice, soup, panchan (spicy Korean vegetables) and water. Three claps of the chukpi and the meal begins. The meal is eaten briskly and in total silence. Once the meal is finished, warm water is brought around and the monks wash their bowls and neatly re-pack them. Since not a single grain of rice is wasted, there is nothing to throw away. Three claps of the chukpi signify that the meal is over and the monks silently file out of the hall.

This daily routine is interrupted once every two weeks, on full and
new moon days, by bath day. On this day the monks shave their
heads in the morning and then in the afternoon assemble in the
main shrine hall to hear a Dharma discourse by the resident Zen
master. Holding his Zen stick in one hand, the master ascends the
podium and the monks prostrate three times. There is usually a
minute or two of silence, which is then broken by a shout or the
sound of the Zen master's staff being rapped against the wood of
the podium. Then the Zen master begins his discourse, which
usually includes anecdotes drawn from the lives of the great

monks of the Zen tradition. Often there will be rhetorical questions thrown at the meditation monks, who usually keep silent in response. The talk usually ends after around 40 minutes, and after prostrating again, the monks return in single file to the Zen hall.

Unlike the Japanese tradition where personal interviews (dokusan) occur on an almost daily basis, there is generally little individual contact between the meditation monks and the Zen master. (If however a monk has some particular question about his practice, he is free to visit the Zen master's quarters.) Of course this means that meditation monks are left to a much greater extent to their own devices in the Korean tradition. They must deal with the feelings of monotony, boredom and restlessness that may arise during the long days of sitting on their own. This greater measure of independence is also reflected in the comparative freedom enjoyed by the Korean Zen monk. In contrast to the Zen monk in Japan, who usually remains in one temple and trains strictly under one particular master with whom he enjoys a fairly close master-disciple relationship, the Korean Zen monk is free to move from temple to temple and train under different masters.

The year is divided into four three-month periods according to the seasons. Each summer and winter there is a three-month intensive meditation period called 'Kyol-che' (tight-dharma) during which the meditation monks are not supposed to leave the temple. Between these periods there is 'Hye-je' (loose Dharma), during which the monks are free to either continue their practice where they are or may wander from temple to temple, seeking instruction from other teachers.

The Korean Zen monk may spend quite a number of years engaged in this routine, depending upon how his meditation practice develops. Usually he will begin in a larger Zen hall belonging to one of the major temples. As his practice develops, he will probably seek out the company of more seasoned meditators, who prefer to remain in smaller Zen halls in more remote mountain locations. Finally, the more advanced meditator will usually choose to remain entirely by himself in a hermitage, where he can sit for longer periods without having to follow the fixed schedule of a community.

There is, however, no fixed progression that the Zen monk is expected to follow. For example, he may spend a number of seasons practicing in Zen halls and then decide to study Buddhist texts, or vice versa. Or he might spend a number of years as the abbot of a temple, only to return to the Zen hall again later. Much depends on his own personal inclination and the manner in which his inner spiritual life unfolds. Although the Chinese 'ancients' advised that Zen should be 'worked out in one go', there is obviously no hard and fast rule on this, and the variations are as many as there have been Zen monks who have devoted themselves to study of the way.

Generally speaking however, as a Zen monk becomes older and more experienced in meditation, other younger monks may gather around him and seek out his instruction. As rumours of his accomplishment and wisdom spread, he may also be invited by lay believers to give public 'Dharma talks'. In this way, through his teaching and the passing on of the Buddhist Dharma to others, he will come to repay the support of the Buddhist community, which he enjoyed during his years of training in the Zen hall. And so, in this way, the 'Wheel of the Dharma' is turned, and a new generation of aspirants receives the opportunity to learn of the 'Great Way' that leads to emancipation from birth and death.

Taewon-sa

Great Source Temple

Taewon-sa on Mt. Ch'onbong is said to have been established in 503 AD by the monk Ado, who came to Paekche from Shilla, spreading Buddhism. At that time he named the temple Chukwon-sa. This story however is somewhat doubtful. In any case, "Ado" seems to have been a generic term meaning "monk", so it is actually possible that the temple could have been founded by any monk at that time.

In 1260 the temple was rebuilt and expanded by National Master Wono Ch'onyong, the fifth abbot of nearby Songgwang-sa. He renamed the temple Taewon-sa, and also changed the name of the mountain from Mt. Chungbong to Mt. Ch'onbong. Master Wono Ch'onyong was fifth in the line succession of no less than sixteen National Teachers who were descended from Master Pojo Chinul at Songgwang-sa.

Chinul's immediate successor was Chingak Hyeshim (1178-1234). Hyeshim passed the civil service examination when he was twenty-three years old. One year later however, after witnessing the death of his mother, he was ordained as a monk. According to tradition, his major realization came whilst he was he was meditating outside on a rock. Apparently, he was so deeply immersed in samadhi that he was utterly oblivious of the snow piling up all around him until he was almost completely buried.

In 1208, two years before his death, Chinul formally appointed Hyeshim as his successor. It was under Hyeshim's leadership that Suson-sa (the original name of Songgwang-sa) really started to blossom as the foremost Zen training center on the peninsula. Later his fame as a Zen master spread far and wide, and many disciples gathered to study under him. It was Hyeshim who compiled the 1,700 Kongans of the Korean Zen tradition into one single volume. This work remains one of the main texts used in the Zen school today.

I sit alone by the old pond;
Suddenly I see a monk in the water.
We look at each other and smile;
I greet him but he doesn't respond.[13]

Chingak Hyeshim

Paengnyon-sa

Temple of the White Lotus

Paengnyon-sa on Mt. Mandok was first established by Zen Master Muyom in 839 AD and called Mandok-sa. The temple however owes its importance to Master Wonmyo Yose, who established the White Lotus Community here in the 13th Century.

Master Yose (1163-1245) was a contemporary and friend of Chinul. He was born to a local official in 1163. At the age of twelve he became a student of Master Kyunjong, of the Ch'ont'ae (C: Tien-tai) school established by Master Uich'on. In 1185, at the age of twenty-three, he passed the monk's examination and then for the next thirteen years he devoted himself to studying the teachings of Ch'ont'ae. In 1198 a major Dharma Assembly was held in the capital which he attended and at which he expounded his ideas. Thereafter he wandered throughout the country with a number of his disciples teaching at many temples.

One day he received a poem from Master Pojo Chinul and a letter inviting him to join the Meditation and Wisdom Community that Chinul was setting up at Kojo-am. Yose ended up staying at Kojo-am (see p.114) for almost ten years practising Chinul's style of Zen meditation until the community

moved to Songgwang-sa (see p.118) in 1200. At this juncture
however he must have felt that Chinul's method was not
helping him to resolve his doubts and that he could not
eliminate the so-called "120 diseases" through Zen practice
alone. The "120 diseases" are the wrong views which are listed
in Master Yen-shu's book, "Zen Secrets of Mind Only" and
which prevent a person from attaining enlightenment.
Accordingly, he returned to his previous Ch'ont'ae practices.

In 1208 at the age of forty-six, while practising the "Sublime Insight of Tien-tai", he finally attained a spiritual illumination in his room at Yaksa-sa on Mt. Wolsaeng. His second illumination came a few years later whilst he was reading Master Chih-li's commentary on the "Contemplation on the Infinite and Boundless Life Sutra". When he came upon the phrase, "The mind makes Buddha, and the mind is Buddha," he suddenly smiled without realizing it.

In 1211, Master Yose established the White Lotus Community at Mandok-sa, since he believed that the Pure Land practices of chanting the Buddha's name and repentance were more suitable for the average person than Zen meditation. Several hundred people from all social classes joined the community. Master Yose himself was a model to all his students. His possessions consisted of three monks' robes and one bowl. He even refused to use a light at night to avoid wasting oil. His daily practice consisted of meditation, chanting the Lotus Sutra, reciting the name of Amitabha Buddha 10,000 times and chanting the Mantra of Avalokitesvara 1,000 times.

When he was about to pass away, his disciple and successor Ch'onin asked him, "If the mind in meditation is already the Pure Land, then where are you going?" He replied, "One thought unmoving, therefore I go without going. He comes without coming. Buddha and sentient beings do not exist outside of the mind."[74]

He passed away in the sitting posture at the age of eighty-three. Posthumously, he was given the title "National Teacher Wonmyo".

Taesung-sa

Mahayana Temple

During the early Three Kingdoms period there is said to have been a four-sided Buddha statue here on this site on Mt. Sabul. In 587 AD, King Chinp'yong visited this mountain and ordered that a temple should be built and that a monk should reside here permanently and make offerings to the Buddha every day. Later, in the 13th Century, the eastern branch of the White Lotus Community was established at this temple by Master Chinjong Ch'onch'aek (b.1206), who was the third-generation successor of Master Yose.

Master Ch'onch'aek, a nobleman, was a descendant of the Shilla royal family. In his youth he studied Confucianism, passing the primary state examination at the age of fifteen and the main examination when he was twenty. Apparently, he felt it was useless to pursue the social status and wealth which could have been his easily, for the next year he was ordained as a monk. Initially, like Master Yose's immediate successor Master Ch'onin (1205-1248), who studied Chogye Zen from Songgwang-sa Master Hyeshim, he studied Zen, contemplating the Hwadu, "Why did Bodhidharma come from the West?" However, at the age of twenty-three he became a disciple of Master Yose. Four years later, whilst writing out a copy of the Lotus Sutra, he had his first realization of the sutra's meaning.

In 1244, Master Ch'onch'aek became the leader of the eastern White Lotus Community at Taesung-sa, which was a community for the people. Religious practice and experience was emphasized rather than theoretical studies. In this respect it was modelled along the lines of Chinul's Meditation and Wisdom Community at Songgwang-sa, although concentration and insight through recitation of the Lotus Sutra was the main practice.

Master Ch'onch'aek himself however seems to have been quite eclectic in his outlook. In 1247 he moved to a small hermitage in the south where he stayed in order to avoid the Mongolian invaders. Then in his later years he retreated to a hermitage called Yonghyol-am (Dragon Place Hermitage) and became known by the nickname "Master Dragon Place". It is probable that during these years he was engaged in practising Zen meditation. This is suggested by a book he wrote called, "The Records of the Precious Storehouse of Zen" which enjoyed popularity during the Koryo Dynasty.

The White Lotus Community continued to exist under the leadership of Master I-an and Master Unmuk during the late Koryo Dynasty. However, when the Ch'ont'ae School was absorbed into the Zen Sect during the early Choson Dynasty, the community disappeared altogether.

Pogyong-sa

Temple of the Buddhist Sutras

When Master Chimyong returned from T'ang China at the end of the 6th Century, he gave King Chinp'yong a collection of Buddhist Sutras that he had brought back with him. He told the king that if he found an auspicious mountain on the east coast, buried the sutras there and built a temple, the country would receive divine protection against attack from the Japanese, and furthermore that it would become possible to unify the peninsula as one country. The king was very pleased to hear this and so, with Master Chimyong, he established Pogyong-sa on Mt. Naeyon in 602 AD.

During the 12th and 13th Centuries, the "Pojo Zen" of Chinul was undoubtedly the main current of Zen in Korea. At that time however there were also other streams flowing through other masters. One such master was Wonjin Sunghyong (1171-1221), who was a contemporary of Chinul. He was ordained into the Huiyang Nine Mountains School at Bong'am-sa (see p.90) but was actually strongly influenced by Chinul's Pojo Zen. He also tried to promote the other, more traditional Nine Mountains teaching styles. From the year 1214, Zen Master Wonjin lived here at Pogyong-sa, expanding it to accommodate his students.

Unusually, Master Wonjin's teacher was actually a layman, Yi Chahyon, whose posthumous title was Chillak-kong (1061-1125), and who was a government official and writer. He resigned his post at the age of forty-eight and lived in retreat on Mt. Ch'ongp'yong. He attained illumination upon reading the phrase, "All things in the world are eyes. Where are you kneeling?" in the Records of Xuefeng.

Unhae-sa

Silver Sea Temple

Unhae-sa was first established by National Preceptor Hyech'ol Kuksa in 809 AD and named Haean-sa. The temple was later renamed Unhae-sa in the 16th Century.

During the 13th Century another teacher who was influential in the Zen community, yet who also did not directly belong to the Pojo Chinul line, was Master Iryon (1206-1289). Iryon belonged to the Kaji Mountain School (see p.72) and did his training at Borim-sa (see p.74). Iryon however, being quite eclectic in his thinking, was not bound by any one particular tradition or school. This is reflected in the breadth of his considerable writings. He was, for example, quite attracted by the Sumi Mountain School, writing various commentaries on the Soto teachings of Master Tung-shan Lian-chieh. However he also drew on the more orthodox teachings of Masters Ch'ing-yuan and Nan-yueh, from whom most of the Korean Nine Mountains Schools were derived, as well as positively accepting the "Pojo Zen" of Chinul.

In 1268, he held a major Dharma assembly here at Unhae-sa, during which he tried to bring about the ideological unification of Buddhism on the peninsula. Significantly, he was concerned to heal the division between the Zen and the doctrinal schools and bring them together under the single banner of Buddhism. Accordingly, he advised his students to, "read the sutras by day and to meditate by night."[75]

Perhaps Iryon's most lasting contribution, however, was his book the <Samguk Yusa> ("Memorabilia of the Three Kingdoms"), which he wrote towards the end of his life while he was at a nearby temple called Ingak-sa. This was a collection of anecdotes, semi-historical and semi-mythological, mainly derived from the Shilla period. Most of the stories are Buddhist in nature and purport to show the intimate connection between the divine protection afforded by Buddhism and the prosperity of the nation. It seems that Iryon's intention was to remind people that Buddhism was the very cornerstone of the nation's identity and political autonomy. This book is considered to be one of the most sacred books of the Korean people.

Chunghung-sa

Re-emerging Temple

One of the most outstanding Zen masters of the Korean tradition, T'aego Pou (1301-1382), was ordained at Hoeam-sa (see p.158) at the age of thirteen by Master Kwangji of the Kaji Mountain School. T'aego was one of the three Zen masters in the 14th Century who are credited with introducing the Chinese Lin-chi[76] school to Korea and it is from T'aego that most of the later Zen lineages in Korea claim their descent.

T'aego lived at a time of considerable political instability, which saw the millenarian revolts across China, the demise of the Yuan Dynasty, and its replacement by the Ming dynasty. On the Korean peninsula, as a figure with a high public profile, T'aego witnessed first-hand the final years and break-up of the Koryo Dynasty. As National Teacher, T'aego was responsible for the establishment of the Chogye Zen Sect[77]. This merged into one the Nine Mountains Schools, which had by now become divided by faction-fighting and power struggles.

During his youth T'aego travelled to various temples, studying Buddhism under different teachers, until at the age of nineteen when he was given the Kongan: "Ten thousand things all return to the one; where does the one return to?" At the age of thirty-three, while staying in Kaesong, the capital, he achieved a breakthrough. At that time he wrote:

I drank up the Buddhas and Patriarchs;
And all the mountains and rivers,
Without using my mouth.[78]

His second and decisive breakthrough came five years later at the age of thirty-seven whilst meditating on the Mu Kongan: "Does a dog have Buddha nature?" "No." At that time he wrote:

After breaking through the solid gate,
The clear wind blows from the beginning of time.[79]

When he was forty-one, T'ae-go came to Chunghung-sa temple on Three Corners Mountain, which is just north of present-day Seoul. The temple itself was probably originally constructed some time during the early Koryo Dynasty (918-1392) but it was T'aego Pou who, as abbot of Chunghung-sa, renovated and expanded it. Many students hearing of his reputation as a Zen master gathered here to study under him. Today, however, nothing remains of the temple.

T'aego-sa

Hermitage of the Great Ancient

I n 1346, T'aego went to North China hoping to meet the eminent teacher Zhuyuan. Most likely T'aego was looking for a Zen master who could confirm that his realization was complete. This would seem to indicate that at that time in Korea there were no Zen masters of sufficiently high attainment. Zhuyuan however had already passed away by the time T'aego arrived, so instead he travelled to the south and called on Zen Master Shih-wu, who was thirty years his senior and an 18th-generation successor of Lin-chi I-hsuan. Shih-wu recognized T'aego's attainment and gave him Inka.

After leaving Shih-wu, T'aego returned to North China to the Yuan capital, where he was invited to give a series of public lectures at Yen-king Temple. These were attended by many of the Mongol high nobility, whom he sharply reminded of their obligations to society. Hearing of T'aego's reputation, the Emperor Shun-tsung sent him a gift of a golden robe but instructed the messenger to test him with this question:

"Please accept this gift as a token of the Emperor's esteem. There is however one condition: you must receive it without using your hands."
T'aego replied: "Of course I would be honored to receive it

without using my hands if you'll first hand it to me without using your hands!"[80]

In 1348 T'aego returned to Korea and for four years lived by farming on Mt. Sosol, most likely due to the political upheavals of the time. In 1352 he was summoned to the capital by King Kongmin. When the latter assumed the throne in 1356, T'aego was appointed Royal Teacher. It was during this period that he attempted to restore harmony to the much-splintered Buddhist community by forming the Chogye Zen School. Then in 1357, against the king's wishes, T'aego left the capital, probably to avoid political intrigue, and returned to Mt. Sosol.

Between 1362 and 1368, T'aego taught at Bong'am-sa on Mt. Huiyang and at Borim-sa on Mt. Kaji. From 1371 he was abbot of Shilsang-sa, and at the age of eighty he was again given the title of National Teacher, this time by the new king. T'aego passed away in 1382 and was given the posthumous title "Zen Master of Perfect Realization".

After T'aego passed away, a stupa was erected in 1385 near this small hermitage on the mountainside above Chunghung-sa (which no longer exists), where he used to come to meditate and write.

Letter from Master T'aego to Layman Sajae

Realizing that impermanence is swift and that the question of birth and death is an important matter, you've come to inquire about the way. This is laudable. However let me ask you in return, who is the one who is aware of impermanence and who is the one who is asking about the path? If you can understand this directly then as we say in our school: "The aspect is unusual; the light shines in the ten directions." However do not get caught on this phrase and try to conceptualize about its meaning. The more you think about it the further away you will get. Rather take hold of the Hwadu and try to come to grips with it.

I'm sure you've heard the case: A monk asked Chao-chou: "Does a dog have Buddha nature?" Chao-chou said, "No!" What did Chao-chou mean? This "No" is not the No of existence nor is it the No of non-existence. It does not denote nothingness either. So tell me what did he mean by this "No"? If you understand as soon as the word "No" is mentioned then you are through. If you are in the least bit unsure of yourself then you better take this "No" and contemplate it in the place where your doubt persists. Whether walking, standing, sitting or lying, twenty-four hours a day just maintain your awareness of it. Steadily keep going in this way looking into Chao-chou's "No". If you continue like this then eventually you will break through and see Chao-chou face to face. At that time go and find a Zen Master to receive confirmation of your understanding.[81]

Ch'onch'uk-sa

India Temple

The origins of this temple at Manjang Peak on Mt. Tobong are attributed to Master Uisang in the 7th Century, but more likely it was established by one of his followers around 673 AD. At that time it was named Okch'on-am. In the 14th Century, during the last years of the Koryo Dynasty, an Indian monk named Chigong visited this temple and remarked to Zen Master Naong Hyegun (1320-1376) that the place reminded him of Yongch'uk Mountain in India. Thereafter the temple was renamed Ch'onch'uk-sa (India Temple).

Master Naong Hyegun (1320-76) was a contemporary of T'aego who also did much to introduce the Lin-chi style of teaching to 14th Century Korea. When he was twenty, he witnessed a neighbour dying and asked an old man in the village, "Where do we go after we die?" The old man was unable to answer. After this, he began to puzzle seriously over the mystery of life and death. Soon after, he was ordained as a monk under Master Yoyon of Myojok-am on Mt. Sabul. After his initial training period was completed, he moved to Hoeam-sa (see p.158), where he attained a spiritual awakening in 1344.

In 1347 he went to Yuan in China, where he studied under Zen Master Chih-k'ung (d.1363) at the Fa-yuan Temple for a number

of years. After receiving Inka from Master Chih-k'ung, he travelled to the Ch'ing-hui Temple where he met Zen Master P'ing-shan Chun-lin, a 19th-generation successor of Zen Master Lin-chi I-hsuan. Their meeting is recorded as follows:

When Naong arrived, P'ing-shan was seated in the cross-legged meditation posture. Naong took several steps to the left and then several steps to the right.

Then the Master asked, "Where do you come from?"

"From Fa-yuan Temple."

"Who did you meet there?"

"I was with Master Chih-k'ung who just came back from India."

"What was Chih-k'ung doing?"

"He was using a thousand swords every day."

"Forget about Chih-k'ung's swords, show me yours."

Naong quickly hit him with his cushion. Master P'ing-shan shouted: "This thief is going to kill me!" and tumbled down from his seat. Naong lifted him to his feet and said, "My sword can kill a man but it can also bring him back to life!" At this the Master burst out laughing.[82]

Naong returned from Yuan in 1358 and devoted the rest of his life to revealing "that thing which fills the sky and covers the whole earth, and which is always existent to everybody." He was tutor to King Kongmin and taught at temples throughout the country.

Shilluk-sa

God s Yoke Temple

Shilluk-sa on Mt. Pongmi was founded during the reign of King Chinp'yong (579-632) and was originally called Poun-sa.

In 1376 whilst staying at this temple Zen Master Naong Hyegun passed away. It is said that at the hour of his death, ominous-looking black clouds gathered in an otherwise cloudless sky and heavy rain poured down over the temple. After his body had been cremated, numerous sarira were found in his ashes. These were enshrined by his disciples, Kakchu and Kaksong, in a reliquary on a hill on the north side of the temple.

After the passing away of Master Naong, many buildings were constructed, and in 1382 over two hundred of his disciples gathered from all over the country to attend the memorial ceremony of his passing.

In the Great Void

A man may wear a thousand faces.
Yet he always belongs to emptiness.
Who knows the reality in front of their eyes?
When the clouds clear, the autumn moon brightens the sky.[83]

Naong Hyegun

Ch'onun-sa

Hidden Spring Temple

C h'onun-sa, originally named Kamno-sa, was founded in in 828 AD by Zen Master Togun. Many eminent monks have practised meditation at this temple and the personal altar set of Zen Master Naong Hyegun (see p.152) is kept here.

A slightly older contemporary of Naong Hyegun was Zen Master Paegun Kyonghan[84] (1299-1375) who along with Masters T'aego Pou (1301-82) and Naong Hyegun (1320-76), is credited with bringing the teachings of Lin-chi Zen to the Korean peninsula. Little is known of his early life other than the fact that he became a monk at an early age. He had no single particular teacher and spent his early years wandering from temple to temple.

In 1351, he went to Yuan China, where he met and received guidance from the Lin-chi Zen Master Shih-wu (one of the teachers of T'aego Pou), whom he credits with teaching him the correct way. As he himself said, "This mountain monk wandered around the south and north of the Yangtze River (in China) and visited all the famous masters there. They all taught students using Hwadus such as 'Mu', 'All things return to the one…', 'What was your original face before your parents were born?', etc. There was no other kind of teaching. Finally I visited Master Shih-wu at Tienhuan Hermitage on Mt. Xiawushan and assisted him for several days. There I learned the 'true teaching of no-mind' which enabled me to completely realize the utmost sublime truth of the Tathagatas."[85] Paegun returned to Korea the following year.[86]

Paegun's illumination came in 1355 while he was reading the following passage from the "Song of Enlightenment" by Chinese Master Yung-chia Hsuan-chueh (665-713):

Do not try to abandon false thoughts.
Do not try to capture the true mind.
The real nature of ignorance is not other than the Buddha nature.
The illusive empty body is the same as the Dharmakaya.

Subsequently he devoted himself to teaching his disciples, declining the order to teach at the royal court. The main thrust of Master Paegun's teaching was the teaching of "no-mind and no-thought":

There is a most sublime means, namely the teaching of no-mind and no-thought. The Sixth Patriarch stated: 'If one does not think at all of good or bad, then one automati-cally enters into the original place. This state is always calm and sublime like the sands of the River Ganges.'[87]

Hoeam-sa

Old Pine Rock Temple

Hoeam-sa was first established by Master Chih-k'ung[88] in 1328, near the end of the Koryo Dynasty (918-1392). It was then renovated by Zen Master Naong Hyegun (1320-76) (see p.152) towards the end of his life. Naong's most famous disciple, Muhak Chach'o, (1317-1407) lived and studied here. Today only the foundations of this once important temple remain. On the ridge to the north of the temple there is a stupa to Zen Master Muhak.

Muhak left home at the age of eighteen and was ordained by Master Soji, the leading disciple of National Teacher Haegam[89] of Songgwang-sa. After studying the Buddhist sutras for a number of years, he came to Hoeam-sa, where he studied Zen under Master Naong Hyegun.

One day Naong asked Muhak: "Chao-chou was once crossing a stone bridge together with another monk. 'Who built this bridge?' he asked the monk. The monk replied, 'Mr. Li Ying'. 'Where did Mr. Li start to build the bridge?' The monk could not reply. Now if I were to ask you the same thing, how would you reply?"

Without saying anything, Muhak formed a stepping stone with his hands. Naong said, "This time you've not been fooled by the Kongan," and gave him Inka.[90]

After this, Muhak lived for some nine years alone in a hermitage on Mt. Solbong deepening his understanding. From then on in his daily life he was said to have been like a great mountain entirely unmoved by events around him. Muhak was appointed as a monk at the royal court of King T'aejo (Yi Sung-gye, r.1392-1398), the founder of the new Choson Dynasty. He also advised the king on the selection of the site for the new capital, Hanyang (present-day Seoul) using the principles of Feng-shui. Indeed, Muhak had a very close relationship with the king and often advised him in times of difficulty.[91]

Zen Master Muhak passed away at the age of eighty while living in the Diamond Mountains. Just before he died, a monk asked him, "When the four elements which constitute the human body separate from each other, where does the man go?" Muhak's final words were:

"The six senses are originally empty.
When the four elements separate, it is just like a dream.
There's no such thing as either coming or going." [92]

Sungga-sa

Sangha Temple

This temple, high up in the Pukhan mountain range, was originally established as a grotto hermitage in 756 AD. It was named Sungga-sa after the monk Sut'ae installed an image of Master Sungga, an Indian monk who was believed to be an incarnation of Avalokitesvara. It is also believed that this was the temple where Zen Master Hamho Kihwa (1376-1433) attained his spiritual illumination. Master Kihwa's name comes from the name of the room where he used to practise meditation, which he called "Hamho-dang", which means the "House of Emptiness".

Before he became a monk, Hamho was a talented student at the Confucian Songgyungwan Institute. However, when he was twenty-one, one of his close friends died. As a result of this experience he was deeply struck by the transience of life. The next year he was ordained as a monk at Uisang-am on Mt. Kwanak in today's southern Seoul. After that he became a disciple of Master Muhak at Hoeam-sa (see p.158), eventually receiving transmission from him and continuing his line of succession.

King Sejong, in the second year of his reign, hearing of the reputation of Master Hamho Kihwa, invited him to teach at the palace. His Dharma speech at the memorial ceremony for the Queen Mother apparently made such an impression on the nobility there that he spent the next four years as teacher to the royal family before he was given permission to leave. Thereafter he travelled widely across the country teaching at many temples.

Hamho wrote quite extensively, the work for which he is best known being the "Comments of Five Masters on the Diamond Sutra". His preface to this work combines elements from both "The Awakening of Faith" by Ashvaghosa and the Zen teachings of the Lin-chi school:

There is "one thing" that has neither name nor form, that penetrates both the past and the future, that lies hidden in one single particle of dust but embraces the six directions of the universe. It contains all mysteries, it adapts to all circumstances. It presides over heaven, earth and humans, and prevails over all beings. It's wider and higher than anything else. Whether we look upwards or downwards, it appears clear. However we hear it, it sounds clear. What a mysterious and divine thing it is! It began earlier than the universe; it has no beginning. It ends later than the universe; it has no ending. What a profound thing it is! What shall I call it? Emptiness or form? I don't know how to name it. It is indescribable.[93]

Hyondung-sa

Hanging Lamp Temple

During the 6th Century an Indian monk named Marahami came to Shilla to teach Buddhism. At that time, King Pophung (r.514-540) had a hermitage built for him on this site on Mt. Unak. During the 9th Century, at the instigation of Master Yongi Toson (827-898), a temple was erected on this site as part of his strategy of protecting the nation through the construction of temples in geomantically propitious locations.

The temple must have fallen into disuse however, because when Chinul (see p.114) was passing through the area in 1204 only the foundations remained. Feeling that this was an auspicious site, he had the temple rebuilt between 1204 and 1211 and renamed it Hyondung-sa.

During the Choson Dynasty it was renovated several times. There is a story that in 1411, Zen Master Hamho was on his way from Samgak Mountain to Oshin Mountain when he lost his way. Suddenly, a beautiful white deer appeared from nowhere. Hamho followed the deer across the mountain and it led him to the site of this now much dilapidated temple. The deer then disappeared. Hamho, realizing that this must be an auspicious site, had the temple renovated and expanded. Today the stele which was erected in 1433 in memory of Hamho can still be seen.

After teaching extensively throughout the country for many years, Hamho finally retired to Bong'am-sa (see p.90) on Mt. Huiyang, where he passed away in 1433.

Hyondung temple high up on Mt. Hyondung.
Mountain stream tumbles down through the rocks.
Cool water flows refreshingly around my feet;
Don't you too want to rest a while on this mountain path? [98]

Hamho Kihwa

Muryang-sa

Infinity Temple

Muryang-sa on Mt. Mansu was originally established by Master Pomil (810-889, see p.84). It is also recorded that Zen Master Muyom (801-888, see p.76) stayed here and enlarged the temple. During the mid-Choson Dynasty, in the 15th Century, Master Soljam (Kim Shisup) resided here for many years.

Soljam (1435-1483) was an official and an outstanding scholar during the reign of King Tanjong. He was strongly opposed to Prince Suyang's usurpation of power, and in the wake of the prince's enthronement as King Sejo, he renounced his position to live the life of a recluse.

Soljam wrote quite extensively, and was an exponent of both Zen and Hwaom. Like Chinul before him he did much to try to reconcile the two schools. In the introduction to his "Annotations of the Avatamsaka Dharma Seal", he wrote that, "Words come from the mind, and the mind is the foundation of the words."

Commentary on the Avatamsaka Sutra by Soljam

"The Dharmadhatu is no more than the real aspect of all beings. The only true condition of the Dharma World is spiritually bright from the origin, unlimited, wide, empty and calm. It does not have a form but it spreads throughout the world. There is no end to it for it contains everything. It is clear to the true eyes of an enlightened one but its characteristics cannot be perceived. It brightens itself within all beings but the reason cannot be understood. Unless one has wisdom's eye to see through truth and the bright wisdom of no ignorance, he cannot see the marvelous and mysterious operation of his own mind."[95]

Taehung-sa

Great Emerging Temple

I t is not clear exactly when Taehung-sa on Mt. Turyun was first established, but it was probably one of the five hundred or so temples established on the advice of Master Toson during the latter part of the 9th Century. By the time of the Japanese invasion of 1592, the records suggest that it had become a fairly large temple. During the mid-Choson Dynasty there were a number of eminent Zen masters associated with this temple. One of these was Pyoksong Chiom (1464-1534).

Pyoksong Chiom's name is derived from the room in the temple where he used to stay, which was called the "Room of the Green Pine Tree". As a young man, Pyoksong Chiom served with distinction in the Northern Expedition of 1491 and was decorated for valour. Soon after this he started to question deeply the value of his achievements. Realizing the ephemeral nature of position and reputation, at the age of twenty-eight he was ordained as a monk at Sangch'o-am in the Kyeryong Mountains. His first breakthrough in his Zen practice came after meeting his teacher, Pyokkye Chongshim.

Little is known about Pyokkye Chongshim, except that in his early life he went to Ming China to study Zen, and became a successor of Master Chong-tong of the Lin-chi (K: Imje-son, J:

Rinzai) school. On his return to Korea, the persecution of
Buddhism was so strong that he was forced to disrobe and live
in hiding with a woman believer who was either his attendant
or de facto wife. He lived on Mt. Hwang'ak and made a living
by cutting and selling firewood.

The story goes that when Pyoksong Chiom met Pyokkye
Chongshim, he asked whether he could study Zen under him.
Pyokkye Chongshim however declined to answer. Pyoksong
Chiom persisted with his requests, and was met with equally

persistent rebuffs. This went on for three years. Eventually Pyoksong Chiom became so frustrated that one day, whilst Pyokkye Chongshim was out cutting firewood, he packed up his belongings and left.

When Pyokkye returned from the mountain he asked where Pyoksong was. The woman who was his attendant said, "He's gone!" Then she rebuked him saying: "Because you were so miserly in your Zen teaching, he left full of anger."

Pyokkye replied: "It's not that I didn't tell him, it's just that he

wasn't listening! Every day I saw him face-to-face and worked and ate with him. Through every action I was teaching him all day long. What else could I possibly give him?"

So saying, he started off after Pyoksong. He climbed a high rock from where he could see Pyoksong walking away and shouted, "Chiom, Chiom!" Pyoksong Chiom turned around surprised and Pyokkye raised his fist and shouted, "I am giving you Zen!" At that instant Pyoksong Chiom achieved his first illumination.[96]

Pyoksong Chiom's second and major breakthrough came in 1509 in the Diamond Mountains while reading the sayings of Master Ta-hui Tsung-kao. He is said to have practised meditation during this period with extreme vigour, sitting in deep samadhi for hours and even days at a time. Afterwards he wandered from temple to temple teaching as he went. In his later years, because of the severe persecution of Buddhism at that time, he retreated to Suguk Hermitage in the Chiri Mountains, where he finally passed away.

Kigi-am

Unique Hermitage

Kigi-am, shrouded in mist during the summer monsoon season and covered with snow in the winter, is located high up on Mt. P'algong. It is one of the several hermitages belonging to Unhae-sa (see p.144) and dates back to the year 816 AD, when it was established as Anhung-sa.

Many eminent monks, including Paegun Kyonghan (see p.156), have stayed and practiced at this remote hermitage. In 1546 it was restored and expanded by Meditation Master Kisong K'waeson. At that time there were around sixty monks who used to train here. Its present form dates back to a later renovation in 1823.

Today there is a small Zen meditation hall here. At the beginning of every summer and winter, around ten to fifteen seasoned meditators still gather to participate in the traditional three-month retreats that have been held here for the past five hundred years.

Emptiness has been full since the beginning;
It will always be that way.
Though it is full,
You won't find a bird's footprint there.[37]

Paegun Kyonghan

Bong'un-sa

Good Fortune Temple

Bong'un-sa, located at the bottom of Mt. Sudo in today's southern Seoul, was originally called Kyonsong-sa and was founded by National Teacher Yonhoe in 794 AD. In 1498 it was renovated and renamed Bong'un-sa.

For most of the Choson Dynasty (1394-1910), Buddhism was strongly oppressed by the Confucian-dominated state. Monks were not even allowed to enter the capital and many of the monastic lands were confiscated. A brief respite came whilst King Myongjong (r.1545-1567) was too young to rule the country and his mother, Queen Munjong, acted as regent. She was a devout Buddhist who tried to protect the rights and interests of monks and actively encouraged the revival of Buddhism. She appointed Master Houng Pou (d.1566) with the task of reviving and reforming the Buddhist Sangha. In 1548 Houng Pou became the abbot of Bong'un-sa, which became the head Zen temple in the country. For a period of about fifteen years there was a brief renaissance in Zen studies, which allowed the torch of Zen to be passed on to a new generation of monks.

When the Queen Mother Munjong passed away in 1565 however, all measures actively encouraging Buddhism were

curtailed and Houng Pou was placed under arrest. In the face
of an overwhelming number of opposing Confucian scholars in
the court who considered him an evil monk, he was forced to
resign his position. He was exiled to Cheju-do, where he was
murdered in 1566. Faced with death he wrote this last poem:

Came as a phantom;
Craziness for fifty years.
Glory and shame are done;
Now the mask is off.[98]

Houng Pou

Koun-sa

Lonely Cloud Temple

Koun-sa on Mt. Tung'un was built in 681 AD and is believed to be another of the temples established by Master Uisang. With the decline of Pusok-sa as the central Hwaom temple, Koun-sa grew, eventually becoming a very large temple of some 360 buildings by the mid-Choson period. During the Japanese invasions of 1592-98, the temple was used as a forward base by the monk militia. Enshrined here are paintings of the legendary figures Sosan Hyujong (1520-1604) and his disciple Samyong Yujong (1543-1610) who, as leaders of the monk militia, are credited with saving the nation from the invading Hideyoshi armies.

Although Master Sosan is most famous for his role in the defense of the nation during the Japanese invasions, his contribution to Korean Buddhism is also worthy of note, for it was his dynamic and charismatic leadership as a Zen master which ensured the survival of the Zen school through the suppression and persecution of Buddhism during the mid-Choson Dynasty.

Sosan was born in the town of Anju in the northern part of Korea. His father worked as a minor government official. His parents were already forty-six years old when Sosan was born,

and they died within a year of each other when Sosan was just nine years old. However, the local county magistrate Yi was impressed by the orphan's keen intellect and adopted him as his own son. When Sosan was eleven, Magistrate Yi sent him to Seoul to study at the prestigious Songgyungwan Confucian Institute. At the age of fifteen, Sosan took the civil service examination but failed. Disappointed and frustrated, he left Seoul, travelling to the south to meet his old tutor. On his way he travelled through the Chiri Mountains region and saw the following statement written on the wall of a temple shrine:

Only those who pass the examination of the empty mind
Can be truly qualified as great men.

This saying made a deep impression on Sosan and he started to wonder seriously what this "examination of the empty mind" was. Shortly afterwards, he was ordained at Ssanggye-sa in the Chiri Mountains under Master Sung'in. After studying Buddhist texts for three years, Master Sung'in said to him, "You are now quite learned in Buddhist sutras but you don't know anything at all about Zen." So saying he sent him to see Zen Master Puyong.

When Sosan met Master Puyong, he told him, "Since I was young I liked to learn, so I've mastered all the Chinese Classics of Confucianism including the Four Books and the

Three Classics. Since I've been a monk, I've read all the important sutras but still I don't know anything about Zen. I just can't seem to understand the phrase, 'Buddha is Mind'. What does it mean?" Master Puyong replied, "It is as you say, the mind that you can't understand." Sosan was only partially satisfied, so he asked, "What is the meaning of Bodhidharma coming from the West?" Puyong replied, I'm busy now, come back and see me after a few days." As Sosan was leaving, the Master suddenly called, "Sosan!" Surprised, Sosan turned around and the Master asked urgently, "What is this? Tell me quick, tell me quick!"[99]

From then on Sosan applied himself day and night to the Kongan, "What is this?" Unfortunately, his practice did not progress well because of his highly intellectual mind. One day he went back to Master Puyong for help. Master Puyong said:

"Zen practice is quite different to ordinary study. All the knowledge and learning that you received before should be discarded. You should give up thinking that you are doing something now. Your mind should be a total blank; you should be like a one-year old baby again. Thus you should devote yourself more to ignorance than to knowledge. It would be wonderful if you achieve realization abruptly on hearing a Kongan of one of the Patriarchs. However this rarely happens. If there is something you don't understand you cannot but help doubting. So devoting yourself to ignorance, that means doubting. If you doubt, that means that at some stage you'll break through that doubt.

"To practise Zen well, you must break through the Kongan of the Patriarchs, and to realize the truth you must cut off the thinking mind. Keep doubting without words or thought. Do it as though you have something stuck in your throat that you can neither swallow nor vomit out. Do it as though you're always thinking of paying off a debt that you owe. Do it as though you're a hen hatching an egg; as though you're a cat watching a mousehole; as though you're a mosquito trying to pierce through the back of an iron horse···"[100]

Some two years later, after strenuous meditation on his Kongan, Sosan achieved a partial breakthrough. At this time he wrote:

Returning from drawing water, I turn my head:
Blue mountains in white clouds without number.[101]

For the next eight years, Sosan continued to deepen his practice staying at various temples and hermitages throughout the Chiri Mountains. One day whilst on his way to a nearby village, he heard a rooster cry and had a further realization. He wrote:

On suddenly reaching my home, everything is just as it is.
The ten million pages of the Tripitika are originally just empty paper.[102]

In 1551, the first monk's examinations in fifty years were held at the instigation of Master Houng Pou (see p.172), who was at that time trying to revive the Buddhist Sangha. Sosan passed the examinations and was appointed the next year as the head of the Doctrinal School. Three years later he succeeded Master Pou as abbot of Bong'un-sa and the head of the Zen Sect. After a few years, however, he resigned his position, and after traveling throughout the country he settled on Mt. Myohyang in the northwestern part of the peninsula. For the rest of his life he remained there, and because of this he became known as Master Sosan, which means "West Mountain". During his stay

on this mountain, he taught and wrote extensively. Over 1,000 students are said to have gathered there to study under him.

The Key to Kongan Practice by Sosan

If you practise any Kongan as sincerely as a hen hatches eggs, as a cat catches a mouse, as a hungry man thinks about a meal, as a thirsty man thinks about water or as a baby thinks about its mother, then you are sure to succeed one day. There are one thousand seven hundred Kongans of the Patriarchs such as: "Does a dog have Buddha Nature?" "Mu."; "What is Buddha?" "The pine tree in the courtyard"; "What is Buddha?" "Three pounds of flax!"; "Dry shit on a stick!" etc. When a hen hatches eggs, the warmth continues; when a cat catches a mouse, its mind and eyes do not move; a hungry man thinking about a meal, a thirsty man thinking about water, or a baby thinking of its mother; all of these thoughts come from the true, sincere mind, not from a false mind. Without this sincerity, in Zen there cannot be any realization.[103]

P'yoch'ung-sa

The Shrine of Outstanding Loyalty
at Taehung-sa

I n 1592, Hideyoshi's army attacked Korea. Within twenty days the Japanese army took the capital, Seoul. King Sonjo fled north to P'yongyang whilst the poorly trained Korean army was unable to offer any resistance. In these dire circumstances, King Sonjo sent a special envoy to Sosan on Mt. Myohyang asking for his advice. Sosan, who was seventy-three years old at the time, immediately offered to field an army of monk soldiers to defend the nation. The king appointed him supreme commander of the monk forces and with the help of Sosan's disciples such as Samyong, a militia of around 5,000 monks was raised. With the assistance of Chinese Ming troops, the monk militia was instrumental in recapturing P'yongyang, and eventually the Japanese were repulsed. The price for this was very high however. Virtually every major temple on the peninsula was burnt to the ground during the invasions of 1592 and 1598. The bitterness lingers to this day.

After the war was over the king as a mark of gratitude bestowed on Sosan the title, "First Zen Master in the Nation and Commander of Zen and Doctrine". Sosan returned to Mt. Myohyang and resumed his teaching and writing. He was very strongly influenced in his approach by the work of Chinul, whose ideas he further developed. Sosan especially emphasized and further elaborated on the Hwadu method of Ta-hui that Chinul had introduced earlier. In his "Handbook for Zen Students", which is a standard text for Zen monks in Korea, Sosan gives detailed and practical instructions on the cultivation of Hwadu-style meditation.

On a cold winter's day in January 1604, Sosan lit incense and called together his disciples for a last sermon. Afterwards he took a portrait that had been made of him and wrote on the back:

Eighty years ago, you were me;
Eighty years later, I am you.[104]

He handed this to his disciples Samyong and Ch'oyong, then seated himself in the lotus position and passed away.[105] The Memorial Shrine to Sosan here at Taehung-sa was built in 1669. King Chongjo (r.1788-1800) named the shrine P'yo-ch'ung-sa, "Shrine of Out-standing Loyalty", and ordered the local magistrate's office to hold memorial services in honour of Sosan every year.[106]

Konbong-sa

West Phoenix Temple

Although today there are just a few buildings marking the site, the records show that during the 15th and 16th Centuries Konbong-sa had some four square km of lands belonging to it, and that there were about seven hundred monks residing here. A temple was first built here in the 6th Century called Wongak-sa, meaning Temple of Original Awakening. The temple was reconstructed and expanded by Zen Master Naong Hyegun (1320-76) (see p.152) in 1358. He renamed the temple Konbong-sa, or West Phoenix Temple, because of a large bird-shaped rock on the western side of the temple.

During the Hideyoshi invasions of 1592 and 1598, Master Samyong Yujong (1543-1610) garrisoned several divisions of the five-thousand-strong monk militia here. Master Samyong also resided here in 1605 after returning from his successful diplomatic mission to Japan to make peace with the Tokugawa Shogunate. At that time, he brought back with him some 3,500 Korean prisoners of war. Like his teacher Sosan, Samyong is a national folk hero for the role he played in repelling Hideyoshi's armies. Myths abound about his activities during the war and his use of magical powers to foil the Japanese.

Samyong was orphaned at an early age and was ordained as a monk at the age of thirteen at Chikji-sa (see p.258). In 1561 he passed the monk's examination in the capital and in 1575 he was offered the position of abbot of Bong'un-sa, the head temple of the Zen Sect, which he declined. Instead he went to Mt. Myohyang to study under Master Sosan. There he became Sosan's leading disciple and received transmission from him.

When the Japanese invaded in 1592, Sosan appointed Samyong as "General of the Monks Forces", and he was directly involved in the recapture of P'yongyang. There is a well-known story about his trip to Japan in 1604 to conclude the peace settlement. One night the door to his room was locked, and the room was then heated from beneath in an attempt to roast him alive. In the morning however, when the would-be assassins opened the door, they found him sitting calmly in the lotus position with icicles hanging from his beard.

Hongje-am

Great Redemption Hermitage

Towards the end of his life, Master Samyong retired to Haein-sa. In 1608 Hongje-am was built for him by King Sonjo in appreciation for his services to the nation. Samyong spent his last years at this hermitage and passed away here in 1610. Although Samyong himself wrote very little, he was instrumental in the publication of his teacher Sosan's "Mirror of Zen" and is largely responsible for its subsequent popularity.

A stupa which contains the sarira of Master Samyong was erected in the year that he passed away. Ironically in 1943, which was towards the end of another period of Japanese occupation, the local Japanese Chief of Police tried to destroy the monument. It was repaired in 1953, but the cracks in the stone can still be seen.

From Mirror of Zen by Sosan

There are three essentials to Zen meditation practice: The first is great faith and confidence. The second is great anger, a strong inward determination. The third is great doubt. If any of these are missing, it is like a cauldron with a broken leg. It becomes useless.

Kongan/Hwadu practice is like a mosquito biting into an iron ox. It does not ask, "Is it like this or that?" It puts its proboscis on the impenetrable, and then, disregarding its own life, it just drives through with the strength of its whole body.

When you practice Zen it is like tuning harp strings which should be neither too taut nor too slack. When you play the harp you can only get a good sound when the strings are tuned correctly. It is the same with Hwadu practice. If you are overly hasty, the blood will become excited. If you forget the Kongan, you'll come to a stalemate. The point is to be neither too hasty nor too slow.[107]

Paengnyon-sa

White Lotus Temple

During the mid-Shilla period, an ascetic hermit monk called Paengnyon who was reputed to have magical powers lived here in seclusion on Mt. Togyu. It is said that when he passed away, white lotuses spontaneously grew from this spot. After his death, during the reign of King Shinmun (r.681-692), a temple was erected on this site and its name commemorates this occurrence.

There is also a stupa dedicated to Zen Master Chonggwan Ilson (1533-1608), who lived here as well. He became a monk when he was a boy and later studied under Master Sosan in the Diamond Mountains. He was one of his most accomplished disciples and dedicated himself to propagating Zen in this region.

Another of Sosan's disciples was the ascetic Ch'ongmae (n.d.). He spent most of his life meditating in a hut beneath Heaven's Peak in the nearby Chiri Mountains. His magical powers were said to have been highly developed. According to legend, one day someone passing by his hut opened the door, only to find him seated facing a wall covered in human excrement. News of this spread and people came from all around to see for themselves. However, when they opened the door to his hut

they were amazed to see that the wall was now covered with
bright and shining gold.

The mountain path is buried in fallen leaves;
There is no one around to ask the way.
An old monk sweeps the leaves;
A child opens the gate and welcomes me in.[108]

Chonggwan Ilson

Paegyang-sa

Nutmeg Tree Temple

Paekyang-sa on Mt. Paegam, which is today a prominent sutra study center, was established in 632 AD by the Paekche monk Yohwan.

Soyo T'aenung (1562-1649), another of Master Sosan's prominent disciples, became a monk here at Paegyang-sa when he was thirteen. Soyo studied under both Master Sosan and Master Puhyu (see p.196). During the Hideyoshi invasions, he was another of the leaders of the monk militia that fought the Japanese. Then during the Manchu invasion of 1636 he served King Injo (r.1623-1649) whilst the royal court took refuge at Suwon Fortress south of Seoul.

Another of Soyo's Dharma brothers was the somewhat eccentric P'yonyang Ongi (1581-1644), who was instrumental in passing on Sosan's lineage to succeeding generations of Zen Masters. P'yonyang was born in the northern town of P'yongyang and was orphaned during the Hideyoshi invasions when he was just eleven years old. After that he left P'yongyang and travelled to the nearby Diamond Mountains, where he went from temple to temple as a beggar. He was ordained as a monk at Pohyon-sa, then a famous temple, and studied Buddhist texts until he was eighteen years old. On completion of his studies he went to Mt.

Myohyang, where he became a student of Master Sosan. P'yonyang received Inka from Sosan in 1603 at the age of twenty-two, during the last year of Sosan's life.[109]

After Sosan passed away, P'yonyang left the temple and returned to a life of wandering. He discarded his monk's robes and was by turn a shepherd, a water-seller and a charcoal vendor. As a shepherd he is said to have driven the sheep to pasture with the cry, "Who am I?" Thereafter he became known as Mr. Who am I? Eventually however he was recognized as Sosan's successor by a woman who had been a follower of Sosan at his temple. After this P'yonyang returned to Mt. Myohyang where he passed on Sosan's line of succession.

The great earth with its rivers and mountains is my house.
Where else should I find my home?
Those who get distracted by the scenery along the way.
Won't find their way home though they walk all day.[110]

Soyo

In today's world we are faced by economic and other difficulties. What kind of mental attitude should Buddhists take during these difficult times?

The present time is a major transitional period in our world history. Science has advanced dramatically so that we have an abundance of materials and products whilst transportation has become much faster and more convenient. People are flooded with all kinds of information to the point where they lose themselves altogether. Consequently, many people entirely lose their mental equilibrium and sense of proportion. Accordingly, most people are encouraged to follow their desires and lead their lives in any way they wish. As a result people have become enslaved by their own desires and are dragged this way and that. When people are led entirely by personal desire, they start to think of other beings as possessions or merely as the object of their desires. The result is selfishness, conflict and general confusion. The most important thing for Buddhists is not to be dragged this way and that by irrational and selfish personal desire.

Modern society, as you indicate, is beset by numerous difficulties and rapid change, so that people seem to be spiritually lost. Isn't there any way to overcome this?

Civilization has entered the age of science and technology. Materially we have developed tremendously in a very short time, so that transportation and information communication has become very fast and convenient. However, at the same time, our world has become very complicated, so that people are losing sight of what is important. As the scientific age advances and life becomes more complicated, people are losing their intrinsic self-awareness. It's impossible to lead a meaningful life without this self-awareness. The solution lies in Buddhism. Buddhism has the complete answer to what is the origin and real identity of the human being. The true self of the human being is not dependent on anything else, and exists in perfect freedom. When a person lives in the embrace of the true self, there is no life and death, there are no barriers, and no good or bad. He is reborn into real life and total freedom. Self-realization will set human beings, who are currently becoming the slaves of technological civilization, free. Everybody should recover their own self-awareness by overcoming the fetters of desire and irrationality. With effort it is possible to uncover the true human being "ch'am saram". Mankind will one day enter a golden age if people can abandon their narrow selfish desires and learn trust each other.

Since you released <Imjerok Yonui> in 1974, you have been emphasizing "muwijinin" Please explain what this means.

The attitude of living attached to material things is mistaken. The person you see reflected in the mirror is only a reflection and not the true self. When people transcend the false self and realize the true self, they overcome such dichotomies as life and death. The person who rests in the original place "ku chari" is free and transcends birth and death. I call this person at the original place "ku chari" the true human being "ch'am saram". Ordinary people can be likened to people living in darkness, while people who have realized the original place "ku chari" are true human beings "ch'am saram".

What is the true meaning of "such'ojakchu ipch'ogaejin" (when you are the master of your situation, wherever you are is ultimate reality)?

When a person resides in the original place "ku chari" he becomes the master of himself; that is, the true self or the original self awareness is restored. In this way he enters the state of complete freedom, which is called "such'ojakchu". Therefore, the person who rests in the original place "ku chari" becomes "ipch'ogaejin".

Please give a detailed explanation of "wi" (position) and "in" (person) in "muwijinin". Is it the body that "in" refers to?

"Muwijinin" refers to "the person without position" (wi). People who take the material world they see as reality cannot live apart from life and death, true and false, and other opposites. "Wi" refers to this mistaken perception. When this misperception is overcome the real inexistence of "wi" becomes apparent. The true self or the "true person of no position" is without birth and death and opposites. This is "in".

Life is an incessant movement, which only the living person is able to witness. So isn't there any way to transcend life and death during this lifetime?

As I said, people, because of their habit of continuous discrimination, create their own delusion which results in their inability to escape from birth and death. When one realizes the true self "ch'am mosup" or the real self "ponnaemyonmok", one can transcend illusion and attain full freedom, where no birth and death exists. When one attains self-realization one becomes "ch'am saram", and when one does not, one falls into the world of opposites; the world of birth and death "saengsagohae". In the absence of such realization, one falls under the delusion of false discrimination "punbyolmangsang" which brings about pain and suffering.

You are a Zen master who has devoted your entire life to Zen meditation "ch'amson". Please tell us why Zen is regarded as important and what Zen really is.

Buddhism has the answer to the various problems of life such as good and evil, life and death. In Buddhism there are many theories. As these theories developed, the most effective way of solving the basic problems of human beings and realizing the true self was sought out. The answer lay in Zen. Zen developed as the best and most efficient way to understand the teachings of Buddhism.

The Kongan was developed in China around 1,200 or 1,300 years ago, but are they still effective in current times?

The ultimate purpose of Buddhism is self-realization. Various methods for people to attain the original place "ku chari" or that thing "ku kot" were developed. Therefore anybody who follows the method correctly can attain realization. The Kongan and Hwadu originated from this background.

May Kongan be created containing the problems or difficulties of the current times?

> Kongan can be limitlessly invented. However, the Kongan that were created and established in China are still used because we can avoid a lot of potential problems by relying on a well-established tradition.

Does that mean that we can create our own Hwadu?

> Yes, absolutely.

Then, why are we not allowed to choose our own Hwadu in our Zen centers?

> It is unnecessary since we already have the Hwadu/Kongans created in China. When something works it should be used. Why fix something that is not broken? The Hwadu that we have are good enough as they are, and so we keep using them.

In society today we see a lot of conflict between religions. What do you think of other religions?

> The attitude that I am right and others are wrong cannot make for a harmonious and peaceful world. We should accept other religions. We should help, understand and respect each other. Only disaster comes from disagreement and conflict.

Who do you think of most often among your Buddhist companions?

> All of them have passed away. Only I remain. But I often recall Songch'ol Sunim, Hyanggok Sunim, and Koam Sunim. Koam Sunim and I were very good friends, and we spent a lot of time together at Paegyang-sa.

Buddhism has influenced Korean society and has been a part of the main stream of Korean culture for around 1, 600 years. However it is now believed that Buddhism no longer has anything to offer. People say that Buddhism is badly in need of reform. What are your thoughts on this subject?

First, the historical flow and evolution of humanity and the reality of the human situation should be clearly and correctly understood. We should realize what the ills are. After that, we should seek the best way to heal the ills of the current times from the Buddhist perspective. Buddhism can once again become a part of the main stream of society when it assumes the role of healing the current ills. It is expected of Buddhists that they will pursue their studies diligently, attain a good understanding of the changes that the world is going through, realize the ills of ordinary people, and then heal them from a Buddhist perspective. But I'm afraid it is not so easy. A lot of study and effort is required.

Biography

Patriarch Seo-ong was born in the town of Nonsan, Korea in 1912. In 1932 he was ordained at Paegyang-sa by Manam Sunim. In 1942 he went to Japan and studied at the Rinzai College. He was appointed the president of Dongguk University Zen School in 1962 and over the next few years he was appointed as Senior Zen master of Tonghwa-sa, Paegyang-sa and Taehung-sa Zen halls. In 1974, he became the fifth Patriarch of the Chogye order. He was awarded an honorary degree of Doctor of Philosophy from the Sri Lanka National Purivania University in 1976. After relinquishing the leadership of the Chogye order, he returned to Paegyang-sa and is still active as the Senior Zen master (Chosil) there. It is said that he has reached a high level of attainment.

Ch'ilbul-am

Hermitage of the Seven Buddhas

The name of this hermitage originates from a legend that in the 1st Century AD, the seven sons of King Kim Suro, the founder of the ancient Karak kingdom, came here to meditate under the guidance of their uncle Master Chang'yu for two years until they became Buddhas. A Zen hall was built here by Master Tamgong during the reign of King Hyogong (r.987-911) of Shilla.

During the 16th Century, Zen Master Puhyu (1543-1608) spent the last few years of his life in retirement here in this very remote hermitage perched high up in the Chiri Mountains. Master Puhyu was a fellow student and contemporary of Master Sosan, and also had a significant influence on the Buddhist community of the time. He was ordained at the age of seventeen, and during the Hideyoshi invasions he took refuge in a cave on Mt. Togyu in Cholla Province. After the war he was accepted at Haein-sa, where he studied under Master Yonggwan, eventually becoming his successor.

Master Puhyu was renowned for his understanding and great virtue. It is said that whenever he received anything from any of his numerous lay followers, he would always give it away. Throughout his life he upheld the precepts of the Buddhist monk and never possessed more than his robe and bowl. By the time he passed away, he had more than seven hundred disciples, the most famous of whom was Pyogam Kaksong (1575-1660). It was the successors of Masters Puhyu and Sosan who kept Zen Buddhism alive amidst the hardships of the 17th and 18th Centuries.

How meaningless the things of this world!
Keep your mind fixed on reality.
If you can enter the empty mind,
The monkey with the six holes will be at rest.[1]

Puhyu

Kongnim-sa

Empty Forest Temple

Originally, National Master Chajong built a small hermitage called Ch'o-am on Mt. Nagyong and lived here during the mid 9th Century. The Shilla King Kyongmun (r.861-875) donated funds, and the hermitage was turned into a temple and named Kongnim-sa.

In 1399 it was restored by Hamho Kihwa (see p.160) and then subsequently expanded during the Choson period. A number of eminent teachers such as Master Puhyu lived and practiced here. Unfortunately, the temple was severely damaged during the Korean War, but has been mostly restored since then. Today there is a small Zen hall here for meditation monks.

At Kongnim Temple

Moonlight falls bright on the snow;
I dream of my home a thousand miles away.
Ice cold wind cuts to the bone;
This wanderer is lost in thought.

Puhyu

Popchu-sa

The Temple of the Teachings

Located on Mt. Songni, Popchu-sa is believed to have been founded in 553 AD by Master Uishin after he returned from India. At that time it was a large temple, consisting of more than sixty buildings and around seventy hermitages scattered across the mountain, with as many as 3,000 monks living here. It is recorded that in the 12th Century, the king gathered 30,000 monks together here to pray for the health of National Teacher Uich'on (see p.110), who was ill. The huge iron pot that was used to feed the assembly still remains. Many of the buildings were burnt down during the Hideyoshi invasion of 1592 but were reconstructed by Pyogam Kaksong around 1624.[112]

Like Samyong before him, Master Pyogam Kaksong (1575-1660) achieved fame as a leader of the monk militia. Pyogam first fought in the Japanese invasion of 1598 and then again during the Ching invasion of 1636. After the wars were over, Pyogam dedicated his time to teaching and to the reconstruction of the many Buddhist temples that had been burnt down by Hideyoshi Toyotomi during the invasions of 1592 and 1598. Besides his reconstruction of Popchu-sa, he also repaired Ssanggye-sa (see p.204) and Hwaom-sa (see p.104), where he passed away in 1660.

One of Master Pyogam Kaksong's most prominent disciples was Such'o Taesa (1590-1668, pen name Ch'wimi), who was a renowned scholar, poet and calligrapher. He was even respected by many of the Confucian scholars of the day. In 1629 he opened a Zen school at Yongch'u-sa.[113]

Nothing more to do: I open my door to the wind.
A monk asks me to explain Zen.
This is what I tell him:
Wash your dinner down with a cup of tea![114]

Ch'wimi

Master Hobaek Myongjo (1593-1661) was a contemporary of Master Pyogam Kaksong and a student of Master Samyong's successor, Songwol-dang Ungsang (1572-1645). He became a monk at the age of thirteen and, like Pyogam Kaksong, he was another of the leaders of the monk militia that fought the Japanese.

When Choson was invaded from the north by the Ching army in 1627, Hobaek Myongjo led an army of 4,000 monk soldiers to victory at Anju and was given an honorary title by the court in recognition of his services. During the second Ching invasion of 1636-37, he helped his country by collecting cereals for military supplies. After the wars, he retired to Mt. Myohyang in the north, where he taught until he passed away in 1661.

Spring's Gone

I gasp for breath in a cloud of dust; everything's ruined.
The 32 years of my life have been a waste.
Last night's wind and rain swept across from West Mountain;
Peach and pear blossoms are gone; spring is on its way out.[115]

Hobaek

Ssanggye-sa

Twin Streams Temple

During the reign of Shilla King Songdok (r.702-737), a monk named Sambop went to China to meet Hui-neng, the Sixth Patriarch of the Zen sect, only to find that he had already passed away. The monk was said to have been so disappointed that he stole the embalmed head of Hui-neng and brought it back with him to Shilla. On his return, he had a dream in which an elderly monk instructed him to look for a place in the Chiri Mountains where arrowroot flowers blossomed in the snow of a fragrant valley. In 722 AD, together with fellow monk Taebi, he founded this temple in the Hwagok Valley, naming it Okch'on-sa, and enshrined the head in a stone reliquary.

In 835 AD, Zen Master Chingam, after returning from T'ang China, rebuilt and enlarged the temple and renamed it Ssanggye-sa. At that time, he built the Hall of the Sixth Patriarch's Head to house this unusual relic. Master Chingam had been orphaned at an early age and later went to China to study Zen. He was ordained in China and remained there for over twenty-five years. When he returned in 830 AD he brought with him green tea seeds, and is generally credited with introducing the cultivation of green tea to this part of the peninsula.[116]

The temple was damaged during the Hideyoshi invasions at the end of the 16th Century and was renovated by Master Pyogam in 1641. One of Master Pyogam's prominent disciples, Paekkok Ch'onung (1617-1680), became a monk at the age of twelve at this temple, and spent some twenty-three years studying here. He was a talented poet and calligrapher whose works were quite popular in their day. However, by this time the threat of foreign invasion was over and the government had returned to its policy of oppressing Buddhism. This oppression intensified during the reign of King Hyonjong (r.1659-1674). Nuns living in the capital were turned out, monks were banned again too, and lands belonging to temples were confiscated by the State.

In the face of this oppression, Master Paekkok Ch'onung was the only monk to go directly before the king to complain about the State's policies. In doing so, he presented a philosophical refutation of all the arguments used by the Confucian scholars to discredit Buddhism. In spite of these efforts however, the oppression of Buddhism continued more or less unabated.

Kumsan-sa

Gold Mountain Temple

Kumsan-sa on Mt. Muak was founded in 599 AD by King Pop of Paekche with the aim of encouraging people not to harm other sentient beings and to live together in peace. It was reconstructed by National Teacher Chinp'yo[117] during the reign of King Hyegong of Shilla (r.765-780) in 766 AD, and became the main center of the Miruk (Skt. Maitreya) faith, the central tenet of which was belief in the advent of the future Buddha. This form of Buddhism was introduced to the Korean Peninsula from China some time during the 4th Century AD.[118]

By the end of the 17th Century, Buddhism was still suffering greatly from persecution by the state, and the valour of the many monks who fought during the Japanese invasions had been all but forgotten. Monks were now at the bottom rung of the social ladder. Zen Buddhism remained secluded in the mountain temples and Zen monks were seldom seen in society at large. Nevertheless, despite the fact that Zen Buddhism no longer enjoyed the patronage of the royal court, cultivation of the Zen way continued, and there remained genuine monks who passed on the Buddhist teachings.

One notable Zen master who lived during this period was

Hwansong Chian (1664-1729). Master Hwansong became a monk at the age of fifteen at Yongmun-sa, where he studied the Buddhist texts and then engaged in Zen training. Little is known of his early life; however as he grew older his reputation as a Zen master spread[119] and his sermons drew large audiences. Around 1725 he held a series of Dharma meetings here at Kumsan-sa, which some 1,400 followers attended. Shortly after this he was framed by certain parties who were envious of his success, arrested and sent into exile on Cheju Island, where he died a week later. His stele can be seen at Taehung-sa (see p.166).

His successor was Hamwol Haewon (1691-1770), who spent most of his life in the Diamond Mountains and passed away at Sogwang-sa[120] in 1770.

About Mind

It is greater than all heaven and earth;
It is everywhere yet it leaves no trace.
Only a fool thinks he can fathom the mind
By measuring emptiness and grasping space.[121]

Hamwol

Unmun-sa

Cloud Gate Temple

Unmun-sa, the largest training center for nuns in Korea, was established in 560 AD during the reign of King Chinhung and was originally named Chakkap-sa. The temple became known as Unmun-sa after King T'aejo, the founder of the Koryo Dynasty, donated farmland to the temple and renamed it Unmun-sa in 937 AD. In 1250, Master Iryon (see p.144) stayed here as abbot and the temple was gradually enlarged throughout the Choson Dynasty.

During the 19th Century the monk most closely associated with this temple was Master Paekp'a Kungson (1767-1852), who was famous both as a scholar and meditation master. He wrote the Zen Manual <Sonmunsu Gyong>, which became one of this period's most important guidebooks on the theory of Zen meditation.

In this book, loosely basing his theory on the dialectics of Chinese Zen Master Lin-chi I-hsuan, he attempted, somewhat controversially, to divide Zen into three different categories. These were: Chosa Son (Patriarchal Zen), which was understanding achieved through the mind-to-mind transmission of the Zen School; Yorae Son (Tathagata Zen), which was understanding achieved on the basis of the scriptural teachings;

and Uiri Son (Rational Zen), which referred to a solely intellectual understanding in which the discriminating mind predominates. According to Paekp'a, whilst Patriarchal Zen and Tathagata Zen both referred to transcendental states, the former was superior.

Master Paekp'a became a monk at an early age and studied under Master Solp'a Sang'on, an eminent sutra master of the day. Paekp'a was such a talented student that by the age of twenty-six he had already been appointed as a sutra teacher. At the age of forty-five however, he realized that his understanding of Buddhism was only at an academic level, so he abandoned his position as a sutra master and dedicated himself to the practice of meditation here at Unmun-sa. By the time that he passed away in 1852, he had achieved renown as both a meditation master and a sutra master.

Ilchi-am

One Finger Hermitage

Master Ch'oui Uisun (1786-1866) was one of the greatest Buddhist scholars of the 19th Century. He was born in Naju, South Cholla Province, and was ordained as a monk at the age of fifteen at Unhung-sa (now Paekdam-sa). Whilst staying at this temple he became mysteriously attracted to Mt. Wolchul (the Moon Rising Mountain), where he attained illumination. When he came down from Mt. Wolch'ul, he went to nearby Taehung-sa on Mt. Turyun (see p.166) and received confirmation of his understanding from Zen Master Wanho Yunu. He then further deepened his understanding, practising at other Zen halls in the area for a number of years before returning to Taehung-sa. Towards the end of his life he built Ilchi-am further up the mountain above Taehung-sa and lived here for more than ten years until he passed away.

Master Ch'oui was friends with many famous scholars and calligraphers of the day and wrote quite extensively. He was most strongly opposed to Master Paekp'a's three categories of Zen. He believed that any classification of Zen according to the superiority or inferiority of the aspirant's fundamental potential for enlightenment could only be detrimental. In his opinion, any differences were conceptual rather than essential.

His works include: Collected Poems, In Praise of Korean Tea, A
Discourse on Zen and The Ilchi Hermitage.

Spring has passed; the mountains are empty.
Sometimes a guest arrives like a cloud.
Comings and goings don't tie me down;
No one knows me; who I am or what I do.[122]

Ch'oui

Mangwol-sa

Moon Watching Temple

Mangwol-sa teeters precariously almost at the peak of Mt. Tobong, just north of today's Seoul. A small hermitage, is believed to have first been built on this site during the 7th Century. In the year 1066, National Master Hyego visited the hermitage and expanded it.

During the late Choson Period in the 19th Century, as interest in Zen declined, chanting the name of Amitabha to ensure rebirth in the Pure Land became a very popular practice amongst Buddhists. At that time many temples had a special hall set aside specifically for this purpose, called the Yombul-dang (mantra chanting hall). Mangwol-sa became a particularly popular temple for this kind of practice. From the beginning of the 19th Century a continuous series of Ten Thousand Day Prayer Meetings were held here. The last of these prayer meetings was held from 1881 to 1908 and was initiated by Master Manhwa.

At the end of the 18th Century a small Zen hall was erected. During the late 19th and early 20th Centuries a number of famous Zen masters taught here, including Masters Mangong (see p.226), Hanam (see p.232), Kumo (see p.258) and Chongang (see p.264). Today the Zen hall still exists and

around thirty monks gather every summer and winter to train here.

Sonun-sa

Zen Cloud Temple

During the final years of the Choson Dynasty there was a famous monk named Master Yongsan (d.1883) who lived at this temple. He was of a very quiet and gentle disposition, and used to wander from temple to temple with just a rug and his bowl, stopping to meditate on rocks or under trees whenever he came upon a good spot. When he sat he would become so absorbed in samadhi that he wouldn't move all day. Sometimes birds would even come to sit on his head. He was also very generous. Whenever he came upon a beggar who didn't have a blanket, he would give him his own. In the villages, he would gather the beggars together and give them food. People called him the 'Captain of the Beggars'. He lived as a floating cloud. Of his own life he wrote:

Heaven and earth:
All is peaceful spring.
Nothing to do in all the directions.
Who other than myself will understand this?

In the morning I boil rice with mountain mist.
I use the moon as a lamp at night:
No one but me does such things! [123]

Before he passed away in 1883, he composed this final poem:

Shadow is the shadow of Yongsan.[124]
Mountain is the mountain of Yongsan.
Where mountains and shadow are not different:
There stands Yongsan all alone.[125]

Tonghak-sa

East Crane Temple

Tonghak-sa, which is today a Zen training center for nuns, is one of the three main temples in the mystic Kyeryong Mountains. There are no precise records as to when it was founded, but it is believed to have been some time in the 8th Century. In the 9th Century Master Toson (see p.100) designated this temple as one of the important prayer sites for national prosperity.

Probably the most significant Zen master of the late Choson Dynasty was Master Kyongho (1849-1912), an eleventh-generation successor of P'yonyang Ongi (see p.188). Kyongho brought a renewed vigour to the Zen establishment, which had lost much of its energy as a result of the persecution and neglect of the previous three-hundred years.

Kyongho lost his father at the age of nine. His mother, left without an income, went to work as a temple cook at Ch'onggye Temple in Kwangju, bringing Kyongho with her. There he was ordained by his preceptor, Master Kyeho, and spent most of his time gathering firewood, carrying water, cooking and cleaning. When he was fourteen he had the chance to study Confucianism and learn Chinese characters from a scholar named Mr. Pak. After a few years his teacher,

Kyeho, returned to secular life and moved up to Seoul, so Kyongho came to live at Tonghak-sa. Here he continued his studies under the well-known sutra master, Manhwa. Kyongho must have been a gifted student, for at the early age of twenty-three he was appointed a sutra lecturer at Tonghak-sa. He was a charismatic speaker and many Buddhist followers would come to hear his discourses.

In 1879, at the age of thirty, however, he underwent an experience that completely changed his life. He was on his way to Seoul to visit his old teacher Kyeho when unwittingly he passed through a small village that had been struck by the plague. Wondering at the absence of people in the streets, he entered a house only to find a number of corpses in various

stages of decomposition. Suddenly he was terrified and realized that all his knowledge was meaningless when confronted with the reality of death. After this, he returned directly to Tonghak-sa and resolved to seek the truth through Zen meditation. He locked himself in his room and meditated day and night on the Kongan, "Before the donkey leaves, the horse has already arrived."

On October 15, 1879, Kyongho's attendant went down to the local village to visit his father who was a lay Zen practitioner. The attendant's father said:

"I've heard that your teacher Kyongho has confined himself to his room and won't see anybody. What are all his students doing?"
The attendant answered, "They are taking it easy."

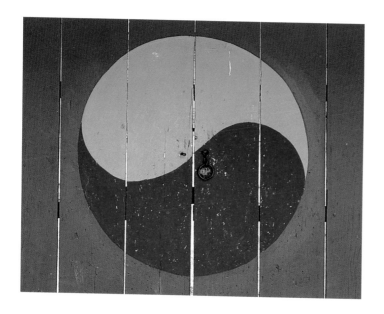

"If they just laze around while eating the food donated by almsgivers, they'll be reborn as cows in their next life!" remarked his father.

"What does it matter if they are born as cows or horses?" said the attendant.

"You shouldn't talk like that," said his father, "or you'll be reborn as an ox with no nostrils!"

The attendant could not understand what his father had said and began to puzzle over what he'd meant by an "ox without nostrils". When he returned to the temple, he asked several other monks, but they didn't know either. Finally, he related the conversation to Kyongho. At that moment, Kyongho burst out of the room shouting, "That's it, an ox without nostrils!"[126] To mark his breakthrough, he wrote:

I heard about an ox with no nostrils.
Suddenly the whole universe is mine.
On the road beneath Mt. Yonam in June,
A farmer who's finished his day's work is humming a tune. [127]

He received Inka and the Dharma name Kyongho (Empty Mirror) from Master Manhwa. Then, in order to deepen his understanding, he moved to Ch'onjang-sa on Mt. Yonam where he continued his practice. At the age of thirty-three he received transmission from Master Yong'am, an eleventh-generation successor of Master Sosan (see p.174).

When Kyongho was in his forties, he set out on a journey around the country, teaching at many of the famous temples such as Pomo-sa, Sangwon-sa, Songgwang-sa and Hwaom-sa where he rekindled interest in the Hwadu style of Zen meditation as taught by Sosan and Chinul. Although his teaching focused on the attainment of realization through Zen practice, he was a very catholic Zen master who held no prejudices against other types of practice such as mantra recitation, chanting, or scriptural study. He believed that Buddha taught people using various means according to their capacity and that therefore all methods were equally acceptable. He emphasized community practice in particular, although not necessarily in the narrow spatial sense of people all being together in one place. He welcomed everyone, whether monk or layperson, man or woman, old or young, wise or stupid, high or low. As he wrote:

"Whoever joins this movement should practise meditation and wisdom simultaneously and go to the Tusita heaven all together. So all of us being Dharma friends, let's all attain enlightenment together." [128]

At the age of fifty-three, he settled at Haein-sa, where he was responsible for the construction of a new hall for Zen meditation. Many students gathered around him. After completion of their training, he encouraged them to go out and establish Zen temples in the towns and villages across the country. In this way he initiated a brief Zen renaissance. His best-known disciples were Masters Mangong (1872-1946), Hyewol (1861-1937), Hanam (1876-1951), Yongsong (1864-1940) and Suwol (1855-1928) who all went on to contribute strongly to the revival of the Zen tradition in Korea.

He was also a gifted poet and calligrapher and left behind quite a number of writings, including essays and sermons which were collected and published by his student Mangong in 1942 as "The Collected Works of Kyongho".

How to Study Zen by Kyongbo

To cultivate the way is no easy task. The life of the Zen monk is not designed for the eating of good food or the wearing of fine clothes, but for the transcending of life and death and the attainment of self-realization. In order to become a Buddha one should examine one's own mind. In examining one's mind, one should reflect that one's body is but a corpse and that all earthly affairs are but a dream regardless of whether they are right or wrong. Life is short and transitory, and upon death man suffers the eternal pains of hell or is reborn as a beast or a ghost. Therefore one should forget about worldly pursuits and constantly investigate one's own mind.[129]

Wolchong-sa

Moon Essence Temple

Wolchong-sa on Mt. Odae was first established by Master Chajang as a small hermitage in 645 AD during his sojourn in this area. Some time after Chajang had passed away, a layman called Shinhyo who was believed to have been an incarnation of Yudong Bodhisattva came to live here as a hermit. Later in the 9th Century, Shinui, a disciple of Pomil (810-889), heard about this and so he rebuilt the hermitage and settled here himself. During the late Koryo and Choson periods, the temple was gradually enlarged. By the late 19th Century it had become quite sizeable, with over a hundred monks in residence.

This was the last temple that Kyongho stayed at before he disappeared from public life in 1903. He was fifty-six years old and had just given a lecture on the Avatamsaka Sutra when he suddenly left without a word. He let his hair grow, and dressed as a layman he wandered north to Hamgyong Province where he settled in a remote fishing village. He is said to have taken ordinary menial work and also to have taught the local children who were illiterate. It is not clear why he left behind the temple life, but probably it was to escape the pressures and expectations of being a famous Zen master. In 1903, just prior to his disappearance, while on his way from Pomo-sa (see p.56) to Haein-sa (see p.62), he wrote the following poem:

A shallow man easily achieves fame in this world.
Wherever he goes he can't find a place to hide.
In fishing village or wine shop:
He is always recognized.[130]

As his life drew to a close he summoned two of his disciples,
Mangong and Suwol, to be with him at the end. Just before
passing away on April 25th 1912, he wrote this final poem:

Light from the moon of the clear mind.
Swallows up the world.
When mind and light are both forgotten:
What is this?[131]

Kimnyong-sa

Gold Dragon Temple

Towards the end of the 19th Century, with the gradual increase in contact between the Korean government and the foreign powers, the oppressive policies against Buddhism that had been the hallmark of the Choson Dynasty began to be slowly lifted. In 1895, as a result of the petitioning of a Japanese monk, Sano-zen-rei, who belonged to the Nichiren Sect, the restrictions on monks entering the capital were revoked by King Kojong (r.1864-1907). The ban had been in force for 272 years. Furthermore, King Kojong allowed temples to be established in the capital. In addition, in 1904 control of Buddhist affairs was relinquished by the Government and handed over to Buddhist monks themselves. Unfortunately, however, all these measures proved to be short-lived.

On August 29th, 1910, Japan forcibly annexed Korea and placed the country under Japanese rule. On July 8th, 1911, the occupation government passed a series of laws which brought the administration of Korean Buddhism strictly under the control of the Japanese governor. The Japanese authorities began the process of trying to promote the assimilation of Korean Buddhism into the Japanese Soto Sect. The country was divided into thirty districts, and thirty temples were chosen as centers from which all the other temples in each region could be controlled. Kimnyong-sa was chosen as one of these main temples.

Founded in 588 AD by Undal Kosa, during the late 19th and early 20th Century Kimnyong-sa became a major Zen training center with over one hundred monks living here and practising meditation. After the Korean War, however, it fell into disuse. By 1989 the buildings were severely dilapidated, several of them being on the verge of collapse, and there was only one monk in residence. Recently a major renovation project has been initiated.

Sudok-sa

Temple of Cultivating Merit

Located on the south side of Mt. Toksung, Sudok-sa dates back to the Paekche Kingdom (18 BC-660 AD). The temple was probably first established during the reign of King Widok (r.554-597) since an ascetic with magical powers named Hye-hyon (570-627) who lived on Mt. Toksung is said to have preached the Lotus Sutra at this temple. The main hall was originally built by Master Chimyong in 599 AD, although the present structure dates from the year 1308. The temple became a magnet for Zen students at the beginning of the 20th Century after Kyongho's famous disciple Mangong (1871-1946) came to live here in 1905.

Zen Master Mangong was orphaned at a young age and became a monk at Ch'onggye-sa when still a boy. From Kyongho he received the Kongan, "Ten thousand things all return to the one, where does the one return to?" After eight years of working on this, he managed to achieve a breakthrough. While staying at Ponggok-sa he had become so completely absorbed in this Kongan that for several days he forgot to eat or sleep. Then one night when he opened his eyes the wall in front of him had disappeared. There was only a single bright circle of light like the moon. Early the following morning as he was listening to the words of the Morning Bell Chant, "The triple

227

world with all the Buddhas and everything in it is created by mind alone," his mind suddenly opened. After this experience he wrote:

The true nature of empty mountain is beyond the million years of past and future.
White clouds and cool wind come and go.
Why did Bodhidharma come to China?
The rooster cries before dawn and the sun rises over the horizon.[132]

After some three years of further Zen practice, he received transmission from Kyongho and came to live on Mt. Toksung where many students gathered to study under him.

Mangong's lasting achievement was his life's work of teaching Zen Buddhism to lay people and nuns. As a testament to his teaching activity, numerous records of his dynamic exchanges with students and other Zen masters who came to visit him still exist.

One day, Mangong and Suwol (another successor of Kyongho) were sitting talking. All of a sudden, Suwol picked up a bowl containing burnt rice and said: "Don't say that this is a bowl of burnt rice. Don't say that it's not a bowl of burnt rice. Just give me one word!" Mangong reached over, grabbed the bowl from Suwol and threw it out the window.[133]

Mangong was also active in his opposition to the Japanese governor's attempts to coerce the Korean Buddhist sangha into following the Japanese style of Buddhism, in which monks were encouraged to marry. On March 11, 1937 the Japanese governor again raised this issue during a meeting with leading monks. Suddenly Mangong struck the governor's table with his fist and let out a deafening Zen roar. He then said, "The universe of ultimate truth is originally clear and empty. Where did the mountains, rivers and the great earth come from? Why on earth should we follow Japanese Buddhism?" From that time on he won the respect of the Japanese governor and his fame as a Zen master spread throughout the country.[134]

In his later years, Mangong lived in a small hermitage above the main temple, which he named "The Hut for Turning the Disk of the Moon". As his time to leave this world approached, he washed himself and sat in the cross-legged position on his meditation cushion. Looking at his reflection in the mirror he exclaimed, "Well, the time has come for me to take leave of you!" Saying this, he laughed heartily and passed away.[135]

Zen Master Mangong's successor at Sudok-sa was Master Hye-am (1885-1985). Hye-am was from a very poor farming family and was completely without education. His father died when he was eleven, so at the age of fifteen, having little other choice, he became a novice monk. When he was seventeen his mother died, and after this he wandered around the country from temple to temple. Then at the age of twenty-three he entered the Zen hall at T'ongdo-sa. During this period he practised with Zen masters such as Yongsong and Mangong. After six years of intense effort, he achieved illumination. He wrote:

"Speech, silence, motion, stillness";
Who dares grapple with this phrase?
Ask me to say something beyond this, I'll say:
A broken bowl can't be put together again.[136]

After this he was appointed abbot of a number of temples, including Sangwon-sa (see p.232) and Ch'ong'am-sa (see p.100). At the age of forty-five, he received transmission from Zen Master Mangong at Sudok-sa. To mark this occasion, Mangong wrote:

Mountains and clouds are neither the same nor different.
Our family has no particular style.
I'll give you Hye-am,
The seal that has no writing.[137]

After Mangong passed away, Hye-am succeeded him as the resident Zen master at Sudok-sa, where he remained teaching until the end of his life. As he got older and older, everyone became curious to know when he was going to die. Eventually one of his students boldly asked him, "When are you going to enter nirvana?" He replied, "When the warm wind comes from the south!"[138] Finally at the ripe old age of one hundred, he passed away. His last words were,

"Impermanence is not empty.
And it's not not empty."[139]

Sangwon-sa

High Place Temple

The site of the present-day Sangwon-sa, deep in the Odae Mountains, marks another of the places where Master Chajang (see p.28) stayed briefly in 643 AD while he was on his forlorn quest to meet Manjusri. It is said that in the year 705 AD two Shilla princes, Poch'on and Hyomyong, came to the Odae Mountains to pray to Manjusri Bodhisattva and built hermitages here. When their father died, Hyomyong went back to the capital, Kyongju, and was crowned king whilst Pochon remained in the Odae Mountains. He established the Chinyowon prayer temple on this site and prayed for Manjusri's protection of the nation.

Later on, in the 14th Century, Zen Master Naong Hyegun's disciple Yongnoam went to the Odae Mountains, and finding the temple in a state of collapse, had it rebuilt. In 1376, thirty-three Zen practitioners began a ten-year retreat here. According to legend, after five years the Buddha statue began emitting rays of light and perfume. In 1465 the temple was rebuilt, and this time more than fifty practitioners gathered here to start a retreat. Throughout the remainder of the Choson period the temple remained active as a place of prayer and meditation. Then, in the spring of 1926, Zen Master Hanam (1876-1951), another successor of Kyongho, came here to live and several hundred students gathered to study under him.

Hanam was ordained at the age of nineteen. Before he became
a monk he is said to have worked as a farm labourer. One day
he watched as another farm worker was brutally beaten to
death by his master. Witnessing this dreadful scene brought
home to him the cruelty and suffering of human existence, and
so he determined to abandon the world. He was ordained at a
temple in the Diamond Mountains where he studied the
Buddhist texts. One day as he was reading the following
passage by Master Chinul, he experienced his first illumination:
If they aspire to the path of the Buddha while obstinately
holding to their idea that Buddha is something outside of the

234

mind or that the Dharma is outside of nature, then even though they pass through kalpas as numerous as specks of dust, burning their bodies, charring their arms, crushing their bones, and exposing their marrow, or else write sutras with their own blood, never lying down to sleep, eating only one meal a day, or even studying the entire Tripitika and cultivating all kinds of ascetic practices, it is like trying to make rice by boiling sand; it will only increase their tribulations.[140]

After this initial awakening, Hanam met Zen Master Kyongho at Sudo-am (see p.250) and asked him for instruction. Unexpectedly, Kyongho quoted a phrase from the Diamond Sutra: "If one sees all forms as non-form, then one can directly see the Tathagata." Upon hearing these words, Hanam felt that in one instant he could see through the entire universe and that whatever he saw or heard was nothing but his own self. After this experience he wrote the following:

The sky is under my feet, the ground is over my head;
Originally there is no inside, outside or in-between.
The lame walk, the blind see;
North Mountain waits for South Mountain without saying a word.[141]

Meanwhile, he continued to deepen his practice, staying at various temples around the country. Then at the age of thirty-five, whilst lighting a fire in the hearth, he attained a final awakening. After this experience he wrote:

I made a fire in the kitchen; suddenly my eyes were lit;
At last the old road has been cleared.
Ask me the reason for the coming of Bodhidharma, I say:
The sound of the well beneath the rock is never wet.[142]

Hanam received transmission from Kyongho and came to reside at Sangwon-sa where he remained for the next twenty-five years until his death. As his fame grew, many students gathered to study under him. Unlike Masters Kyongho and Mangong who were somewhat eccentric in their behaviour, Hanam was very strict about keeping the precepts.

With the outbreak of the Korean War in 1950, the army ordered the evacuation of both Wolchong-sa (see p.222) and Sangwon-sa. Despite the pleas of his students however, Hanam refused to leave the temple, saying that when he had arrived twenty-five years previously he had vowed to remain here until he died. After everyone had left, the Communist soldiers from the north overran the temple. When they saw the master sitting calmly in the meditation posture however, they were so impressed by his utter lack of fear that they left him alone. After fasting for many days, Hanam passed away on March 22, 1951 whilst seated in the lotus position.

Another of Kyongho's disciples who resided at Sangwon-sa was Suwol (1855-1928). He was the oldest of Kyongho's five successors and his story is the most unusual. He came from a very poor family of farm labourers and was completely illiterate.

His family was so poor that there was not enough money for him to marry.

At the age of twenty-nine, having few other options, he applied to become a monk at Ch'onjang-sa, a small country temple. Because of his age, his utter lack of education and his ignorance of Buddhism, the abbot was, not surprisingly, unwilling to accept him. Eventually however he agreed and assigned Suwol to menial work around the temple. At the same time, he gave him a short sutra to repeat as he went about his chores. One day, whilst engaged in his work, he became absorbed in deep samadhi.

A few years later, he came here to Sangwon-sa where he continued his practice. It must have been at this time, around the turn of the century, that he met Master Kyongho and began his Zen training under him, eventually receiving Inka from him. During this period he also resided at Pohyon-sa in the Diamond Mountains.

In 1912 Suwol, together with his Dharma brother Mangong, was summoned to the side of Kyongho before he passed away. After Kyongho's cremation, Suwol then travelled further north, crossing the Yalu River into Manchuria with others who were fleeing from the Japanese occupation forces. There he built a small hut that he called Hwaom-sa and lived from farming. He did not accept any disciples and left behind no successors. He died in 1928 at the age of seventy-four.

Yongt'ap-chon

Hall of the Dragon Pagoda

The Hall of the Dragon Pagoda was founded in 1945 in remembrance of Master Yongsong. Master Yongsong (1864-1940) was another of the successors of Master Kyongho. He is particularly famed for his role in the independence movement that sought to throw off the yoke of Japanese imperialism during the early years of the 20th Century. Master Yongsong is commemorated at this temple in a rather peculiar way: in his late '60s, while he was in the middle of reciting a sutra, one of his teeth fell out. Thinking nothing of it he tossed it aside. That night, one of his disciples saw a mysterious glow in the dark and on further investigation found that the light was coming from the tooth. The tooth is now enshrined in a stupa in front of the hall.

Master Yongsong was ordained as a monk at the age of fourteen at Haein-sa (see p.62). He began his training with the study of the Buddhist texts and the chanting of Kwanseum Bosal's "Mantra of the One Thousand Hands". His first realization came when he was crossing the Naktong River at the age of twenty-three. At that time he wrote:

The moon of a thousand years hangs over Mt. Kumo.
On the Naktong River, the waves rise from far away.
Where does the fishing boat go?
It floats forever on a field of reeds.[143]

After this experience, he wandered from temple to temple continuing his meditation practice. Then when Master Kyongho became the resident Zen master at Haein-sa in 1902, Yongsong received from him the Kongan, "The mountains, rivers and the great earth all have their original source. What is the source of human beings?" After meditating intensely on this, at the age of forty he achieved a major breakthrough. He wrote:

The man who searched for the ox in the forest of the Five Skandas[144]
Sits alone in an empty room inside a single wheel of light.
Who says that there is round or square, long or short?
One ring of fire consumes the many thousand worlds.[145]

In 1910 the Japanese annexed Korea and Master Yongsong became an active participant in the struggle against Japanese colonialism. In 1911 he moved to Seoul and established a small temple named Taegak-sa in Chong-no, central Seoul. This became the main Zen center in Seoul, as well as an important base for the Korean Independence Movement.

On March 1st 1919, a nationwide demonstration against the Japanese occupation was held. At this time Master Yongsong was one of the thirty-three patriots who signed a declaration

proclaiming the independence of Korea from Japanese colonial rule. As a result of his involvement, he was imprisoned for three years at Sodaemun Jail in Seoul. At that time he formulated the ideas which became the foundation of his "Great Enlightenment Movement". This movement was a kind of engaged Buddhism that was far ahead of its time.

He tried to popularize Zen practice and founded quite a number of Zen centers for lay people around the country. At Taegak-sa he established a center for the translation of Chinese Buddhist texts into Korean. Initiating this work was of lasting importance, since most ordinary people were at the time unable to read Chinese characters. Due to his efforts, the Avatamsaka Sutra, the Diamond Sutra, the Heart Sutra and many other Buddhist texts became available in the vernacular for the first time. He also wrote extensively himself, leaving behind a rich legacy of Zen teachings, including: <Su Shim Non> (Thesis on Cultivating the Mind), <Kwiwon Chongjong> (The Stream Returning to its Source) and <Kakhae Illyun> (The Sun Wheel of the Ocean of Enlightenment).

Further, Master Yongsong was also interested in promoting the economic self-sufficiency of the nation. To this end, he established a farming community on the Manchurian border and an orchard at Hadong, where Zen meditation and farming were practised hand in hand.

On February 24th, 1940, Master Yongsong summoned his leading disciples and said: "Well done, you've worked hard; now I must leave you."[146] After this he passed away. He was seventy-seven years old and had been a monk for sixty-one years.

Chonghye-sa

Temple of Meditative Wisdom

Chonghye-sa, which sits high up on Mt. Toksung, dates back to the Paekche Kingdom, when it was established as a small hermitage. Since then many ascetics have lived here. In 1930 Zen Master Mangong enlarged it and built the Zen hall. At that time over one hundred monks were in residence. Today it remains active as a small Zen training center.

Zen Master Hyewol (1861-1937), another of Master Kyongho's leading disciples, was ordained at this temple at the age of eleven. When he was twenty-four he began to practise Zen under the guidance of Master Kyongho. One day Kyongho was giving a lecture in which he quoted the following passage from Chinul's "Secrets on Cultivating the Mind": "The four elements, or in other words, the physical body, can neither preach the Dharma nor hear the Dharma. Only One Thing within you, without form but singularly bright, can preach the Dharma and hear the Dharma. What is this One Thing that is without form and singularly bright? This thing is the nature of all Buddhas, and also your own original mind."[147] Upon hearing this, Hyewol experienced an illumination. He continued his studies under Master Kyongho for a number of years, eventually receiving Inka from him.

Master Hyewol was rather unusual in that he never learned to read. Consequently he did not study Buddhist texts, spending his time instead doing manual labour around whichever temple he stayed at. He particularly liked clearing land so that it could be used for cultivation. Despite this, he never missed a chance to teach others.

Whenever Master Hyewol preached a Zen sermon, he used to begin by saying: "I have two swords. One is the sword which kills men and the other is the one which brings them back to life. Do you understand what kind of swords these are and when I will use them? Be careful for when you meet my sword, you'll lose your life!" A Japanese army general who disliked Buddhist monks heard about this. One day he went to the temple where Hyewol was staying and brandishing his sword he challenged Hyewol saying: "I have heard that you have a man-killing sword and a sword that brings men back to life. Show me your sword or I will kill you instantly with this!" Hyewol smiled without showing any fear or surprise and said: "All right, if you'd really like to see my sword I'll show it to you." The general proudly replied; "Well then, let me see it!" "Look over there right behind you!" said Hyewol. The general turned round to take a look. As soon as his head was turned, Hyewol struck him three times on the neck in rapid succession with his hand shouting: "Here is my sword!" The general was so surprised that he fell over. Henceforth, recognizing Hyewol's spiritual strength, the general treated him with the utmost respect.[148]

Towards the end of his life, after teaching at a number of temples, Master Hyewol retired to a small temple on the outskirts of Pusan. During the 1930's, a visitor to Master Hyewol recorded the following story:

"When we entered Anyang Hut, a shabbily clothed old man followed us into the guest chamber. As we bowed before him, he returned our greetings and asked us, even before we could sit down. 'Do you know what can be seen harmoniously and what can be heard harmoniously?' My companion answered in the negative and the aged priest said nothing more. The following

*morning, as I was reading a newspaper, the old man came to me
and again asked. 'Do you know the meaning of…?' I replied that
all was alike, whilst drawing a rectangle on the newspaper with my
finger and another rectangle in the reverse way. He again made no
remark.*

*That night we stayed nearby and then called on the old monk
again in the morning. On our way we brought a few pears which
we now peeled for the old man and which he ate gratefully. When I
asked him whether the ondol (heated floor) was warm enough, he
replied that when heated it got warm! I again asked him if he had
enough blankets. He replied: 'Namu Chongsung Kuwang Taesin' (a
meaningless phrase). I presume that he wished me to cease my
nonsensical dialogue.*

*Staying with him for a few days. I tried to fathom his daily life and
manners. I noticed that he received a stranger and a disciple who
had studied under him for years in exactly the same way. It was as
though I saw in him for the first time a man who had completely
overcome all feelings of intimacy. I once read a discourse calling
for the negation of distinction between intimate and remote and
wondered how a man could possibly reach the state in which he is
free from all feelings of intimacy. However, as I observed the daily
life of this great monk, I instantly realized that this task was within
the reach of every man if he diligently attended to his religious
practices. Although it would be impossible for my dull vision to
pierce the depths of this great priest's mind, I felt that I had now
liberated myself from all prejudice, concepts, discernment and
narrow knowledge. To me his every act was a precious sermon.*"[149]

Master Hyewol passed away at Anyang Hut in 1937, at the age
of seventy-seven.

Paekdam-sa

Temple of One Hundred Ponds

Paekdam-sa, nestled deep in the Sorak Mountains, dates back to the 7th Century when it was apparently established by Master Chajang (see p.28). At the end of the 8th Century, the temple was rebuilt and renamed Unhung-sa. Over the succeeding centuries the temple was reconstructed a number of times. In recent years the monk most closely associated with this temple was Master Manhae (1879-1944), who is remembered both as a poet and for his role in the March 1st Independence Movement of 1919. His ideas of freedom and equality laid the foundations for the passive resistance and non-violence of the independence movement.

Manhae was ordained at Paekdam-sa in 1905 at the age of twenty-four, and spent many years living here. During his twenties, he wandered around Manchuria and Siberia as a mendicant and also went to Japan in 1908, visiting various temples in Tokyo and Kyoto.150 When Korea was formally annexed by Japan in 1911, it was Manhae who provided the ideological and philosophical nourishment needed by the Korean Independence Movement in their struggle against Japanese oppression. For Manhae, at the core of the Buddhist teachings was the concept of freedom, the meaning of which unfolds as one progresses towards the realization of one's

Buddha nature. So in this sense, freedom is the birthright and intrinsic nature of all human beings. As he wrote in his "Abstract of Thoughts on Choson Independence":

"Freedom is the life of all things and peace is the happiness of life. Therefore, a person without freedom is dead and a person whose peace is taken from him is a man of despair. The circumstances of a suppressed man are the same as a tomb, and the surroundings and the whole life of a person who has to struggle all the time are nothing but hell. Therefore the foundation of happiness in this world is freedom and peace. And in order to achieve freedom people are prepared to surrender their lives as though they were as worthless as dust; to sustain peace they are willing to accept any sacrifice. This is a statement both of the right to live and life's responsibility."[15]

Pyoch'ung-sa

The Temple of Outstanding Loyalty

P'yoch'ung-sa on Mt. Chaeyak is believed to have been originally established by Master Wonhyo (see p.40) in the 7th Century. In 826 AD, during the first year of the reign of Shilla's King Hungdok, a travelling Indian master was inspired by some auspicious-looking clouds floating above this mountain to build a three-storey pagoda here to enshrine some sarira of the Buddha. It is also said that while he was staying here, the Indian master cured the third son of King Hungdok of leprosy. The temple was renamed P'yoch'ung-sa when a shrine was built here in 1839 in honour of Master Samyong (see p.182).

One of the most remarkable Zen masters of the modern era passed away at this temple in 1966. Master Hyobong (1888-1966) was born in P'yongyang, and after studying law at Waseda University in Japan became the first Korean judge during the colonial period. After practising as a judge for some ten years a case arose in which he was forced to sentence a fellow countryman to death. After this, without giving notice even to his family, he disappeared, earning a meager living as a wandering toffee seller. Three years later, at the age of thirty-nine, he entered a temple in the Diamond Mountains and was ordained as a monk. Once he entered the meditation hall, he was given the "Mu" Kong-an, which he meditated on with extreme determination, never lying down to sleep. He was called the "Wheat-Pounder Monk" because he always sat straight and strong like a wooden wheat-pounder. When he was forty-three, he built himself a small hermitage where he practised in total solitude for

one-and-a-half years. Finally he attained a major realization. At that time he wrote:

At the bottom of the ocean, a deer hatches an egg in a swallow's
    nest.
In the heart of a fire, a fish boils tea in a spider's web.
Who knows what is happening in this house?
White clouds float westward; the moon rises in the east.[152]

After this Master Hyobong emerged from his retreat and became a widely respected and notoriously strict Zen master, teaching at a number of famous temples. In 1958 he was appointed Patriarch of the Korean Zen Order. On May 14th 1966, here at P'yoch'ung-sa, he passed away while seated in the meditation posture. His final Nirvana poem reads:

All the teaching of my life
Was just like a sixth finger on my hand.
Ask me about today's event and I'll answer:
The round moon is shining over a thousand rivers.[153]

Sudo-am

The Hermitage of Cultivating the Way

This very remote hermitage high up on Mt. Puryong dates back to the Unified Shilla period (668-935). The two stone pagodas in front of the main hall are thought to have been built in the year 857 AD by Master Toson, who established the nearby Ch'ong'am-sa (see p.100).

Master Hyobong's best-known disciple and successor was Zen Master Kusan (1909-1983), whose vision and energy enabled Songgwang-sa to regain its place as the foremost Zen training temple in the country. Master Kusan was also the first master in the Korean Zen tradition to invite Western students to train in a Korean temple.

Master Kusan was born in 1909 into a farming family in Cholla Province in the southwest of the peninsula. From an early age he had an innate curiosity about Buddhism. He studied Confucianism at the local school until he was fifteen and after that worked as a barber while also helping out on his parents' small farm. Suddenly at the age of twenty-six he contracted a severe illness. One day, while he was sick, a friend of his who was a Buddhist layman asked him, "Since the self-nature is originally pure, where is your illness?" These words had a major impact on Kusan who decided to go to a small temple in the

Chiri Mountains to recite the mantra of Avalokitesvara, "Om mani padme hum", for one hundred days. Upon completing this retreat, he found that he was completely cured of his illness. Three years later he decided to become a monk, and was ordained by Master Hyobong who gave him the "Mu" Kongan to work on.

After entering the Zen hall, Kusan practised with determination. He spent a number of years practising both in Zen halls and alone in hermitages. Eventually his practice became so strong that even when he lay down he would not sleep and his Hwadu would remain brightly with him at all times. Of this period he wrote: "At this time when I was hungry, I would find something to eat; when thirsty, I would drink; when the room was cold, I would light a fire under the floor. I tried to practise as hard as I could and would sleep very little."[154]

Kusan's first breakthrough came when he was practising here at Sudo-am hermitage after meditating for seven days continuously without lying down to sleep. A fellow practitioner and friend had just died and Kusan had resolved to achieve an awakening before his friend's memorial cere-mony. However, Kusan later wrote that he did not consider this experience to be a true awakening.[155]

Bulil Sonwon

Buddha Sun Meditation Center
(at Songgwang-sa)

In 1943, Master Kusan moved to Haein-sa, where his teacher Hyobong was the resident Zen master. He stayed there for three years practising in a small hermitage. In 1946 he experienced another breakthrough, after entering a state of samadhi in which for fifteen days he completely lost any sense of the objective world. He wrote:

The front of the mirror is dark.
The back is bright and clear.
The front is not the front, the back is not the back.
When front and back are shattered, the mirror is complete.[156]

After the outbreak of the Korean War in 1950, Haein-sa was overrun by Communist forces. Masters Hyobong and Kusan both managed to avoid capture and fled to the south near Pusan. After the war, Kusan received Inka from Master Hyobong. At that time, Hyobong wrote:

I planted the stump of a plum tree.
Due to the old wind flowers have already blossomed.
Without fail you will behold the bearing of fruit.
Therefore bring me the pit of the plum![157]

In 1957, feeling that his understanding was still not complete, Kusan once more went into retreat. After a further three years of hard practice, he experienced another breakthrough. At this time he wrote:

Penetrating deep into the core of Samantabhadra.
Manjusri is seized and defeated; now the great earth is quiet.
It is hot on this mid-winter's day and the pine trees are so green;
The stone man riding a crane is flying over blue mountains.[58]

When Kusan presented this to his teacher Hyobong, he received transmission. Hyobong said, "Until now you have been following me; now I shall have to follow you!"

In 1969, Kusan became the resident master of Songgwang-sa (see p.118) and initiated the rebuilding of Suson-sa, the Zen hall. In 1970, regular Zen training resumed. The next year Master Kusan visited the United States, and the first foreigners interested in Zen practice began to arrive in Korea. In 1973 Bulil International Zen Meditation Hall was opened in a special compound within the precincts of Songgwang-sa.

In October of 1983, Kusan composed his Nirvana poem:

The autumn leaves covering the mountain are redder than spring
flowers;
The universe reveals its great power.
Life and death are both void;
Absorbed in Buddha's ocean-seal samadhi, I depart with a smile.[159]

On December 16th, seated in the meditation posture, Zen Master Kusan passed away leaving behind no successor to his Dharma. His final teaching was:

Samsara and Nirvana are originally not two;
As the sun rises in the sky it illuminates the three thousand
worlds.[160]

The nature of the entire universe is nothing other than your own mind. All things are created by the mind and arise from it. So where is the creator of the universe? Your own mind alone is the creator.

There is no one else who created it for you; therefore, this universe is your own universe. This is true whether you are awakened or not. The universe can be affirmed or negated only because we are here right now. If we were not present, there would be no one to make such affirmations or denials. Since we create the universe, how can one then say that we came from anywhere or will depart to somewhere else? In reality there is neither coming nor going. This is the truth.

There are no doors or gates that open to the Great Way. You can neither enter it nor leave it. Throughout, the Dharma worlds are as numerous as the sands along the River Ganges, there is not a single thing that is not permeated by it. It is also called the "secret store of the Tathagata". There is no movement within the highest truth. It

neither decreases nor increases. Throughout the worlds of the ten directions every single phenomenon is completely permeated by all phenomena. Hence, this truth is also called the "Ocean of Wisdom".

The radiance of the subtle principle, with which all beings are endowed, is extremely brilliant. Whether raising your hands, moving your feet, putting on clothes, or eating food; in every action it is clear and distinct. The subtle functioning knows no limits. Thus, the mountain's being high, the ocean's being vast, the flower's blooming, the bird's singing, and each thing's being long *or short; there is nothing that is not the true nature. Upon awakening to your true self, you are called a Buddha; upon forgetting your true self you are called a sentient being. Human life is very short. It doesn't last forever. Who else is there to blame if you live your life in vain without awakening to your true self?* [161]

Zen Master Kusan

Chikji-sa

Temple of Direct Pointing at Mind

Chikji-sa, in the foothills of Mt. Hwang'ak, is said to have been established by the Monk Ado, who brought Buddhism to Shilla in the 5th Century. The temple was rebuilt by Master Chajang (see p.28) in 645 AD. Then in the 16th Century, Master Samyong (see p.182) was ordained here. During the Japanese invasion of 1592, the temple was completely burnt down, but was subsequently rebuilt in the 17th Century. In recent times, Master Kumo (1896-1958) was resident Zen master here for over twenty years.

Zen Master Kumo was ordained at the age of sixteen at Mahayon Temple in the Diamond Mountains. He learnt from a number of eminent Zen masters including Masters Kyongho (see p.216) and Hyewol (see p.242), and around the age of twenty-six he achieved his first awakening. Two years later he met Zen Master Powol, a disciple of Zen Master Mangong (see p.226), to whom he presented this poem:

I see through this illusory world:
There is neither is nor is not.
Everything is like this:
No matter how hard you try to find the root, you'll only find
emptiness.[162]

Master Powol recognized his awakening and Kumo became his student, studying under him for two years. Before he could receive transmission from him however, Powol passed away, so Zen Master Mangong gave him transmission on Powol's behalf. At that time Mangong wrote:

Under Toksan Mountain,
I'm now transmitting the formless stamp.
While Kumo is flying across the sky,
Powol is landing under the cinnamon tree.[163]

After his awakening, Kumo sought out the company of beggars. They taught him that the beggar's life is simple and that there are only three rules: First, never complain about the poor food;

second, don't complain about your ragged clothes; third, don't expect a luxurious bed! After receiving this advice, Kumo lived as a beggar for two years testing his Zen insight in everyday life.

He then retreated to a hermitage for one year to further deepen his practice, and after that spent the next few years wandering through the Chiri Mountains with only his robe, bowl and a tent, practising wherever he chose. At the age of forty, he became the resident Zen master here at Chikji-sa, where he remained for twenty years instructing the many students who gathered to study under him. He also taught at Hwaom-sa (see p.104). He passed away on October 8, 1968, at the age of seventy-three.

According to Kumo, enlightenment has two aspects. First, there is the understanding and insight that comes through the experience of living itself. And second, there is the inner awakening that can be achieved through the practice of sitting meditation. Kumo believed that both were essential to achieve a thorough and penetrating insight. He constantly stressed the need to test one's understanding through everyday life and was very much opposed to theoretical Zen.

Kumo gave his students the "Mu" Hwadu and told them: "If you hold onto your Hwadu then you're alive. If you let go, you're dead. If you don't awaken to its meaning, your mind's eye will remain blind and you'll be forever frustrated. Always reflect back on your own mind; otherwise you'll be distracted by externals and you'll never reach your original home. Then you won't find freedom and you'll just end up caught in misery."[164]

Kungnak-am

Paradise Hermitage (at T'ongdo-sa)

Zen Master Kyongbong (1892-1982), became a monk here at T'ongdo-sa at the age of fifteen after the death of his mother. Having completed his initial training, he began his Zen studies under Zen Master Hyewol (see p.242), but did not find any affinity with Hyewol's teaching. Leaving him, Kyongbong went to Haein-sa (see p.62) and then to the Diamond Mountains in the north where he practised Zen meditation at a number of temples for several years.

It was at Kungnak-am that he experienced his first awakening during a Hwaom Dharma Assembly. At that time he wrote:

Only the most astute can swallow heaven and earth.
The stone monkey rides on the back of a crane following the clay
*   tortoise.*
The bird sleeps in the forest of flowers where the silent mountain
*   river flows.*
Who can appreciate the arrowroot vine moon and the breeze
*   through the pine trees?[165]*

He wasn't satisfied with this initial breakthrough, however, so he took up the Hwadu, "What is this?" and continued his meditation practice. On November 20, 1927, at two o'clock in the morning, he experienced his second awakening when he saw the flickering of the candle in his room. He wrote:

I've been looking for myself all this time.
But the one I've been looking for has been here all along.
Ha! On meeting myself, this time there's no more doubt;
Flowers bloom and the whole world flows.[166]

After this experience he continued to deepen his practice and corresponded often with Masters Yongsong (see p.238) and Hanam (see p.232). In 1949 he became abbot of T'ongdo-sa and in 1953 became the resident Zen master at this Zen hall. He remained here for thirty years accepting and teaching all who came without discrimination.

Just before he passed away, one of his students asked him: "After you depart from here, I'd like to be able to see you. What is your real appearance?" Master Kyongbong kept silent for a while and then looking around he smiled and said, "In the middle of the night, try to reach for the bolt on the front gate."[167]

Yongju-sa

Dragon Jewel Temple

Yongju-sa is said to date back originally to the Shilla period. During the latter part of the Choson Period, in 1789, King Chonjo (r.1776-1800), decided to move the tomb of his father Changjo, who was tragically murdered while still the crown prince, from Sangju to nearby Suwon. At that time, he entrusted the monk Pogyong with the task of reconstructing this temple and dedicated it to the soul of his departed father. The story goes that on the eve of the temple dedication ceremony in 1790, King Chongjo dreamt of a dragon ascending to heaven with a jewel in its mouth. The temple was therefore renamed Yongju-sa, which means "Temple of the Dragon with the Jewel". In 1969 Zen Master Chongang Yongshin (1898-1975) established a Zen training hall here.

Master Chongang lost his mother at the age of seven and was taken in by his stepmother. She ran away shortly afterwards, however, leaving him alone with nowhere to go, and he was forced to sell pottery in the streets to survive. A monk found him and took him to live at his temple, and then at the age of sixteen he went to Haein-sa, where he received ordination. After eight years of intensive Zen practice in Zen halls around the country, he finally broke through the "Mu" Kongan at the age of twenty-four. At this time his awakening was certified by both Masters Hyobong (see p.248) and Hyewol (see p.242). At twenty-six, he went to Sudok-sa and received recognition from Mangong (see p.226). One evening, as he was standing outside looking at the sky, Master Mangong asked him: "The Buddha attained awakening on seeing the morning star. Of all the stars above which is your star?" In reply, Chongang got down on all fours and started looking for his star amidst the dust on the ground.[168]

Chongang was resident Zen master at a number of temples, including Pomo-sa (see p.56) and Mangwol-sa (see p.212), before establishing the Zen hall at Yongju-sa. On January 13, 1975, sitting in the meditation posture, he asked, "What is life and death?" Then he shouted, "Ho!" and a few seconds later he passed away.[169] Zen Master Chongang was succeeded by Master Songdam, through whom the spirit of his teaching still survives.

Songdam was also orphaned at a young age. During the Korean War, Master Chongang worked as a street-seller to provide for him and to pre- vent him from being drafted into the army. Eventually, Songdam received Inka from Chongang, and currently tea- ches at Yonghwa-sa near Inch'on.

Naeso-sa

Rare Appearance Temple

Naeso-sa, which stands at the foot of Kwanum peak, dates back to the Paekche Kingdom. It was built in 635 AD by the monk Hyeguduta and was originally called Sorae-sa. The existing structures were built in the 17th Century. The name is believed to have been changed to Naeso-sa during the early part of the 19th Century.

Zen Master Haean (1901-1974) became a novice monk here at the age of thirteen. It is said that he liked the sound of the temple bell early in the morning and this attracted him to the monk's life. At seventeen he went to the nearby Paegyang-sa (see p.188) and studied sutras under the renowned Sutra Master Manam (1876-1951). Two years later, in 1918, he entered the Zen hall at Paegyang-sa. He received the Hwadu, "Penetrate iron cliffs and silver mountains" from Master Hako, the resident Zen master. After seven days and nights of intensive practice, he heard the sound of the moktak calling everyone to dinner and, "iron cliffs and silver mountains all fell down." He wrote:

Hearing the sound of the moktak, chukpii and bell.
The phoenix flew over the silver mountain.
Ask me about the good news, and I'll say:
In the dining room there's a bowl overflowing with rice.[170]

Two years later Haean left
Paegyang-sa and travelled
through Manchuria and China
for three years. He spent two
years studying Buddhism in
Beijing. After returning to
Korea, he devoted himself to
teaching at a number of temples before retiring to Naeso-
sa. At the age of seventy-four
he announced the date of his
departure from this world at a
Dharma meeting in Seoul.
Then on March 9, 1974, after
morning yebul, he is reported
to have said, "Now is a good

time for me to leave, it's quiet and there's no-one around." He
repeated the Buddha's words, "Don't rely on others, work out
your own salvation," and passed away.[171]

Although he had previously intended to enter Nirvana on March
7, his birthday, this turned out to be the day after a seven-day
retreat and the temple was still crowded with people. He
therefore delayed his departure until the 9th, so as not to
inconvenience others. His Nirvana poem was:

Where birth and death can't reach,
There is another realm.
When we take off these old shabby clothes,
The moon shines bright.[172]

Tonghwa-sa

Temple of the Bright Paulownia Tree

Tonghwa-sa on Mt. P'algong was founded by the priest Kuktal in 493 AD and was originally called Yuga-sa. In 832 AD, it was rebuilt. At that time a paulownia tree in the main courtyard began to blossom in the middle of winter, and so the temple was renamed Tonghwa-sa. The existing buildings date back to the 18th Century, when the temple was mostly reconstructed. During the 20th Century a number of eminent Zen masters taught at this temple, including Masters Hyobong (see p.248) and Hyanggok (1912-1978).

Hyanggok became a novice at the age of sixteen and was ordained at Pomo-sa when he was twenty. Thereafter he entered the Zen hall at Naewon-sa under the guidance of Zen Master Unbong. One autumn as the wind was blowing through the valley, it pounded against the Zen hall door, making a tremendous noise. At that moment Hyanggok broke through his Hwadu. He went to tell Zen Master Unbong.

Unbong said, "If you've awakened give me one word!"
As soon as he said that, Hyanggok hit the wooden floor.
"Not good enough!" said Unbong, "You'll have to try harder if you want to open up your mind."
Hyanggok retorted:

"One thousand words, ten thousand words,
A dream within a dream.
That's all this is;
All the Buddhas and Patriarchs have deceived me."

Zen Master Unbong was filled with delight and gave him Inka.
He said:

"Because there's nothing to give and nothing to receive,
There's no stamp of the Patriarchs.
If we surpass the law of non-giving and non-receiving,
Then the black crow and the rabbit won't walk together
anymore."[173]

After receiving recognition of his awakening from Master
Unbong, Hyanggok continued to deepen his meditation
practice. One day while staying at Bong'am-sa (see p.90), a
fellow meditator asked him, "You can see the live person when
you've killed the dead person, and you can see the dead
person when you bring him back to life. What can you do?"
Hyanggok was unable to reply. Thereafter for twenty-one days,
he practised meditation so intensely that he even forgot to eat
or sleep. One night he experienced another awakening. He
wrote:

Suddenly when I saw my two hands it all became clear;
Three generations of Buddhas and Patriarchs are but the flower of
*   my eye.*
The one thousand sutras and ten thousand sayings, what are all
*   these?*
The Buddhas and Patriarchs also lost their bodies and lives.

Just one smile at Bong'am-sa gives lasting pleasure for a thousand
*   years.*
A few tunes on Mt. Huiyang signify nothing to do for a long, long
*   time.*
Next year too, there will be a big round moon;
Where the golden wind blows, the crane's cry is forever new.[174]

From that time on, Hyanggok could not be fooled by any Zen questions. He taught at a number of temples, including Tonghwa-sa, and Bulguk-sa (see p.26), and gave Inka to his successor, Zen Master Jinjae[175] in 1967. Three days before he passed away on December 5, 1978, he wrote:

The stone woman dances beside the stream.
I step out even further than the first Buddha.
The universe shines bright with infinite clarity;
This is my eternal reward.[176]

Paengnyon-am

White Lotus Hermitage (at Haein-sa)

Paengnyon-am is the highest of all the hermitages belonging to Haein-sa. Many masters have lived here over the years though it is Master Songch'ol (1912-1993), the much revered patriarch of the Chogye Order, with whom this hermitage will always be associated.

Master Songch'ol was married at an early age and had one daughter. At the age of twenty-four however, becoming profoundly aware of the impermanence of life, he left his family and was ordained as a monk. After completing his basic training, he practised meditation with total dedication at Bong'am-sa (see p.90) and Taesung-sa (see p.140). It is said that for eight years he never lay down, even sleeping in the lotus position. Later he lived for some ten years in total isolation at a hermitage on Mt. P'algong studying the Buddhist sutras. From 1967 until his death, he lived in relative seclusion here at Paengnyon-am.[177]

Somewhat paradoxically, although Master Songch'ol claimed to be but a simple mountain monk without any learning, he was extremely well-informed on many subjects and his library contained more than 6,000 books. Reportedly he could speak six languages and he was a regular subscriber to Time Magazine.

Questioner: The worldwide illusion that materialism can bring happiness and meaning to life is gradually collapsing. Where should contemporary man turn in order to find meaning in life?

Songch'ol: Man's true value lies in his innate existence, not in materialism. To correct the distorted ideas which are circulating today first requires the recognition of man's basic dignity. Fundamentally, man is absolute. He is eternal, unlimited and absolute. But materialism is ruining his dignity, his sense of worth and his values.

However once you clean a dusty mirror, there's nothing else you need do. It performs its function just as it should. There is nothing to save and there's nothing to seek. So what is necessary is to recognize man's absolute nature and his sense of human dignity.[178]

Clarifying the Stages

When we're talking about the issue of awakening and supreme enlightenment how can we know what it is? What yardstick can we have for determining whether someone has reached this state? Well actually, in the "Ten Stages Discourse" of the Avatamsaka Sutra, we find very clear standards concerning this issue.

If we look at the stages of meditation in Buddhism, the first is called "maintaining clear movement"; that is to say, whatever your activities in daily life, you should be maintaining an even awareness. You have to maintain this constantly and evenly, without disruption. At this stage however, one cannot continue to meditate while sleeping and therefore one dreams.

Being able to continue the meditation through the dreaming state is called "maintaining in dreams". In the "Ten stages Discourse" we find:

"At the seventh level of Bodhisattva development, one has no obstruction in dreams, and can study at one's will."

This is referring to meditation. If one falls asleep during meditation and can still concentratedly study in one's dream, then one has reached the seventh level. A Bodhisattva who has reached this level can continue to meditate in dreams, although this may not be

possible if he falls into a deep sleep. But there is a level where this is
possible even in a very deep sleep. Again we find in the "Ten Stages
Discourse":

"It may look as though the Bodhisattva is sleeping, but really he is
not."

No matter how deep his sleep, his mind is still clear as if he were
wide awake. If one can keep this mental state of clarity all the time,
through waking and sleeping, then one has reached the level of
complete freedom that is beyond the eighth level of Bodhisattva
development. This level of complete freedom, however, may take
either of two forms.

In the first form, if one retains complete clarity even in dreams, yet still has remains of the tiny, troublesome delusions from the Alayavijnana[179], then one is a freely-moving Bodhisattva above the eighth level. In the second form, however, if one has eliminated these delusions completely, one will make contact with ultimate reality, and then one is said to have reached the level of Tathagata.[180]

Songch'ol

Questioner: What is the Way?

Songch'ol: The Way is the basis of the universe and it is the essence of everything. It is absolute, and it transcends time and space whilst at the same time embracing time and space. Each thing in itself is the Way and the present reality too is the absolute. Man has the Way within himself, within his heart. So if you discover Mind as it really is, you will see the Way for yourself.

However, people can't see their own mind because it is covered with delusion, in the same way that dark clouds block out the sun. The sun is there all the time, but in order to see it the clouds must clear. In the same way, if you wish to see Mind you have to rid yourself of your delusions.

Questioner: What is realization?

Songch'ol: Once all illusion has been swept away, then that is the state of self-realization. In this state there is not even a trace of illusion having been swept away. This is the state of "No Mind". You may think that "No Mind" refers to intentience like a rock or a tree, yet this is a complete misconception. The state of "No Mind" is the Great Light of Wisdom that is all embracing, eternal and constantly abiding. This is the Bhutathata, the essence of life itself.

Most people fall into unconciousness when they're asleep, but the realized person has the Great Light within himself constantly, no matter how deep he sleeps. Such a state is evidence of having attained realization.[181]

Magok-sa

Hemp Valley Temple

There are two stories about the founding of Magok-sa on Mt. T'aehwa. According to the first version, it was founded by Master Chajang (see p.28) in the year 643 AD. The second version claims that it was founded by Zen Master Muyom when he returned from T'ang China in 845 AD. The second version seems more credible in view of the fact that the Nine Mountains temple Songju-sa (see p.76), where Muyom taught, is nearby.

During the 11th Century the temple fell into disuse. It is said that when Pojo Chinul (see p.114) was passing this way, he discovered a band of robbers living here and chased them off. Thereafter, with assistance from the king, the temple was restored.

The current structure of the main hall dates back to the 17th Century. During the late 19th and early 20th Centuries, both Masters Kyongho (see p.216) and Mangong (see p.226) taught here at various times. It was also here that a second-generation successor of Mangong, Zen Master Seung Sahn, was ordained in October 1948.

Zen Master Seung Sahn needs little introduction to the English-speaking Buddhist world. Since he first arrived in the United States in 1971, he has been one of the most active forces in the spread of Zen Buddhism in the West. In contrast to the sometimes rigid and frequently severe Zen of other schools, with his great warmth, humour and contagious "can-do" spirit, he brought a Zen that was at once accessible, down-to-earth and relevant to people's everyday lives.

Consequently, from the humble beginnings of one small Zen center that he established in 1972 in Providence, Rhode Island, his energy and indefatigable spirit have spawned an international network of Zen centers called the "Kwan Um School of Zen". As one of the pioneers in spreading the

teachings of Zen Buddhism in the West, his life's work will no
doubt be looked upon by future generations as having been of
great historic significance.

Seung Sahn was born in 1927 during the Japanese colonial
period, in a small town close to P'yongyang, the capital of
today's North Korea. His father was an architect and the family
owned an orchard. While still at school, Seung Sahn joined the
Korean underground independence movement in their struggle
against the Japanese. Then, after the surrender of the Japanese

in 1945, he went to Seoul and enrolled at Dongguk University, only to find himself suddenly cut off from his family, who lived north of the 38th Parallel. Amidst all the political and emotional turmoil of the times, Seung Sahn considered how he could best help his country. One day a friend gave him a copy of the Diamond Sutra. Upon reading the words, "All things that appear in this world are transient. If you view all things that appear as having never appeared, then you will realize your true self," he determined to become a Buddhist monk.

After ordaining here at Magok-sa, Seung Sahn went up into the mountains to begin a grueling one hundred day retreat. He recited the <Shinmyo Janggu Dae> Dharani (The Great Dharani) for twenty hours a day, eating only pine needles dried and beaten into a powder. He relates that for the first forty days he was constantly assailed by doubts. Then after fifty days he began to have terrifying visions. After seventy days these hallucinations became visions of delight. Finally on the ninety-ninth day, as he was outside chanting and hitting his moktak, his body completely disappeared and he found himself in space. From far away he could hear the sound of his own voice and the beating of the moktak. After returning to normal body consciousness, he realized that the rocks, the river and everything he could see and hear was his own true self. The next day he wrote:

The road at the bottom of Mt. Wongak is not the present road.
The man climbing with his backpack is not the man of the past.
Tok, tok, tok, his footsteps transfix past and present;
Crows in a tree; caw, caw, caw! [182]

It was here at Magok-sa that Seung Sahn met his teacher Zen Master Kobong (1890-1961), a disciple and successor of Master

Mangong (see p.226). Zen Master Kobong had a reputation for being brilliant but somewhat unorthodox. He liked to drink wine and he only taught nuns and lay people since he considered monks to be too arrogant and lazy.

Kobong became a monk at the age of twenty-one. After wandering from temple to temple, he became a student of Master Mangong at Chonghye-sa (see p.242) in 1922. Subsequently he became the attendant of Master Hyewol (see p.242). There is a story that has been passed down from Kobong's period of training under Master Hyewol: One day a farmer who lived nearby brought some rice to the temple as a donation. Since it had been raining heavily, the farmer, the horse and the rice were all soaking wet. Master Hyewol decided to test his students and asked them each to write a single Chinese character that "never gets wet even when rained on". Some students wrote the character for mind, some for wind, some for Buddha and some for sky. However, each time Hyewol shook his head and said no. Finally Kobong wrote the character for rain. When Hyewol saw this he looked at Kobong and smiled.[183] Soon after this Kobong received Inka from Master Hyewol.

When Master Kobong arrived at Magok-sa in the spring of 1949, Seung Sahn received instruction from him. Kobong advised him that attaining final enlightenment is difficult through mantra practice. "A monk once asked Master Chao-chou, 'Why did Bodhidharma come from the West?' Chao-chou replied, 'The pine tree in the courtyard.' What did he mean?" asked Kobong. Seung Sahn understood but did not know how to reply so he said, "I don't know." Kobong said, "Keep this mind that doesn't know. This is true Zen practice."[184]

A year later, in January 1950, Seung Sahn formally received transmission from Zen Master Kobong. Kobong wrote:

Dharmas do not appear.
Dharmas do not disappear.
This is the Dharma of non-appearance and non-disappearance.
Its name is Paramita[185]

Hwagye-sa

Shining Stream Temple

Hwagye-sa, a small temple on the outskirts of Seoul, was established during the Choson Dynasty in 1522 when a hermitage called Podog-am was moved to this site and renamed Hwagye-sa. Today the temple includes an International Meditation Center.

After the Korean War (1950-53) Zen Master Kobong became quite ill so Seung Sahn brought his teacher to Hwagye-sa, where he became abbot. Seung Sahn looked after his teacher here until 1961, when he passed away.

During the 1960's Seung Sahn established a small temple in Tokyo for Koreans living in Japan and then in 1971, hearing of the growing interest in Zen amongst Westerners, he left for the United States. Since that time he has taught throughout the world, spreading his own unique style of Zen teaching.

Don't Know Mind by Zen Master Seung Sahn

"If you keep Don't Know mind, there are no opposites. So there's no Western, no Eastern, no American, no Korean, no Taoism, no Christianity, no Zen, no life, no death, no good, no bad, no name,

no form, no God and no Buddha. That name is Primary Point. Primary Point is absolute. Everything comes from Primary Point and returns to Primary Point. What then is Primary Point? Primary Point's name is Don't Know. Don't Know mind means cutting off thinking. To cut off thinking means to be at the place before thought arises where there's no speech and no words.

How is one to keep this Don't Know mind? When a mother sends her son to war, even though she works, eats, talks to her friends and watches television, she always keeps in the back of her mind the question, 'When will my son return home?' Keeping Don't Know mind is the same as this. While working, while eating, while playing, while walking and driving, always keep the question, 'What am I?'[48]

Shinwon-sa

Temple of the New Age

Located on the south side of the mystic Mt. Kyeryong (Dragon Egg Mountain), Shinwon-sa was founded by Koguryo Master Poduk in 651 AD. During the 10th Century, Shinwon-sa was one of the temples selected by Master Yongi Toson (see p.100) to be reconstructed for the purpose of promoting national prosperity through the protection of Buddhism. The temple was subsequently renovated a number of times over the years, notably by Zen Master Muhak (see p.158) in 1393. During the 19th Century, the Chinese characters denoting the name of the temple were changed by Confucian scholars from "Temple of the Garden of the Gods" to "Temple of the New Age", though the transliteration remains as Shinwon-sa.

In 1982 extensive renovation work was undertaken and the Kwan Um International Meditation Hall was opened here for winter retreats. The last international meditation retreat was held here in the winter of 1999, and in the autumn of the year 2000 a new International Zen Meditation Center was established nearby at Musang-sa, on the other side of Mt. Kyeryong.

Pictured here is the "Central Mountain Altar" of Mt. Kyeryong, which was constructed at the end of the Choson Dynasty

during the reign of King Kojong (1864-1907). It is one of three main mountain shrines on the Korean Peninsula. The "Upper Mountain Altar" is on Mt. Myohyang in the north whilst the "Lower Mountain Altar" is in the Chiri Mountains in the southern region of the peninsula. According to Feng-shui experts, these are the three most important energy centers that sustain the Korean nation.

With the development of science and technology it seems as though humanity is gradually suffocating itself. There seems to be more distrust in the world than ever before and people are gradually becoming more and more isolated and alienated from each other. Human beings are even described by some as mechanical robots living under the yoke of modern society. Dissatisfaction appears to be growing and people are losing what inherent self-awareness they possess. What has made the human being, who ought to be the master of his/her destiny, become like this? What can be done in order to address the problems facing modern society? What role can Zen play in curing the disease of this age? This dialogue on the theme of 'Modern Civilization and Zen' took place between Zen master Seung Sahn of Hwagye-sa and Songbon Sunim, a Professor of Dongguk Buddhist University, in an effort to identify the problems faced by modern society and offer possible solutions to them.

Songbon Sunim: Modern civilization seems to be confronted by five critical problems: war, shortage of food, overpopulation, destruction of the environment and the loss of humanity. Each issue is interrelated, but particularly the loss of humanity appears to be the cause of escalating social problems. It is believed that Buddhism directly addresses these issues. Would you begin with your thoughts about war?

Seung Sahn Sunim: Wars are caused by changes in the balance of power in the world. There are different realms of powers which all interact in this world: the power wielded by humans, the power associated with the animal kingdom and the power of nature itself. Of these, the power wielded by mankind has become the most dangerous. It must be evident to all, that mankind is currently responsible for most of the damage being inflicted on the earth.

Within the human realm, it can be seen that the egoism of personal desire is starting to control most of society. Throughout the 19th and 20th Centuries, ideology played an important role in controlling society. However, since the early 1990's, with the advent of the age of free market capitalism, it is evident that this is no longer the case. Humans are now the slaves of economics. Human beings are starting to resemble dogs, cattle and horses in that their only concern is survival. So human beings are becoming even worse than animals. Animals at least only attack other animals out of necessity when hungry, but humans behave much worse than that even though they are already satiated. War is brought about by this kind of human being.

Collective egoism in society seems to be growing irrespective of nationality, religion or political persuasion. Perhaps collective egoism can be viewed as another kind of war at the national level. And as the fire of this egoism rages we see the human being change into an economic animal. How can this issue be addressed by Buddhism?

Humans have two kinds of power, the inherent and invisible power within the mind and the externally directed power to act in the world. When humans focus solely on the material world without, then the outer world becomes collectivized and organized. Grouping together and fighting for food, results in war. It is from this that I think, the destruction of human nature originated. Forming groups for self-protection and fighting each other is the way of animals. This problem can be cured when the true nature of mankind is uncovered. The world was not created for humans only. So in order to live in harmony in this world, the mind of great compassion needs to be generated. In the absence of this quality of mind it is not possible for all living beings to co-exist in peace. For example, animals that are butchered to satisfy people's greed will only be reborn again carrying with them the seeds of war and revenge. The only way to overcome this is to work towards the collective self-realization of mankind.

The world religions of today can be divided generally into two kinds in terms of geographical environments and climates. The religions and philosophies which originated from India and China are categorized as the 'religions of the forest', whilst the monotheistic religions which originated from the Middle East such as Judaism and Islam are categorized as the 'religions of desert'. The East seems to emphasize the harmony of both humans and nature while the West tends to emphasize their division and separation. Humans and nature are believed to be inseparable in the 'religions of forest'. Accordingly there is the conception of 'all things as one'. So humans tried to live their life in the knowledge that they were an integral part nature. In the 'religions of desert' on the other hand, a god as absolute maker of the world was created. So people came to believe in and follow this only god, creator of all things, not accepting the existence of other gods or beings. As I see it, the problems of modern society stem from this religious tradition with its dualistic thought structure.

Yes, I believe that you are right. There is no past in the religions of the West. They are heading merely from the present to the future. This blocks people from seeing mankind as a part of nature. On the other hand, Buddhism admits the past, the present, and the future. The present is the result of the past, and the future is the result of the present. When we view things in this way, the balance of the world and nature will be preserved in the correct manner.

This dualistic foundation of Western religion, which has the tendency to analyze and divide, seems also to be carried through into Western science. Western science, in which the dissecting and analysis of things is regarded as its purpose, tries to break down things which simply cannot be broken down. For example, living things once broken down into their composite parts will obviously no longer be living things. I think that this is the biggest weakness of modern science. Also I think that the analytic, dualistic way of thinking is the cause of much of the confusion in the world today.

Actually, it is a fact that Buddhism also divides and analyzes. But the difference is that Buddhism proposes a way to return to the origin. This point is illustrated by the Hwadu: "Ten thousand things all return to the one; to where does the one return?" As you know well, this Hwadu comes from a dialogue between Zen master Chao-Chou and another monk. This Hwadu clearly expresses the East Asian idea that the root of everything is one.

Furthermore, this Hwadu provides a direct insight into the very essence of Zen and East Asian thought. That is to say, the idea that by emptying oneself and completely immersing oneself in nature, one can find oneness with the universe. Also it raises a profound question about the origin of existence. 'The ten thousand things' symbolize the positive attributes of affirmation, existence, differentiation and the real aspect of phenomena. On the other hand 'the One' represents the ideas of negation, emptiness, non-differentiation and equality. So you can appreciate that Buddhist philosophy also involves an element of analysis and division. However underneath all this, the underlying intent is always the return to the origin.

On the contrary, in Western philosophy one finds the roots of modern society with its obsession with specialization and fragmentation, which is leading to the systematic mechanization of mankind. So human beings are losing their essential humanness or humanity. Although this is taking place, the damage is not necessarily irreversible. A way back is possible but not through any paradigm offered by Western philosophy. Only Buddhism and Zen can offer real solutions.

The difference between Eastern and Western philosophy is also reflected in the different approaches taken by Eastern and Western medicine. Eastern medicine is essentially preventative in nature, seeking to protect and strengthen the weaker organs of the body, while Western medicine is reparatory in nature focusing on the surgical removal of the weak and sick parts. A parallel can be drawn in the different concepts of freedom and peace. In the East punishment consists of exile from society to create a kind of mental freedom. However, in the West punishment consists of confinement, which focuses on the limitation of spatial freedom. So one can see that in the East there's the pursuit of mental and inner freedom and peace while in the West there is the pursuit of material and outer freedom and peace. Many scholars believe that if society is to evolve in the future, mankind must focus on the Eastern concept of inner mental freedom.

Yes absolutely, I agree. This is not just a passing trend. Many Western scholars are feeling the limitation of their own studies, and are exploring the Eastern approach through Zen practice. This shows the limitation of the Western philosophic approach. Why do you think scholars with Ph.D.'s are becoming involved in Zen? It's because they are blocked. They are not finding the breakthroughs and solutions that they expected through the Western paradigm. Just as Zen monks do Zen practice to cut through the discriminating mind, they are taking up Zen practice in order to find a way to break through their doubts.

Many scholars are convinced that the principles of Buddhism will be an important instrument in future philosophical studies as well as in bringing about world peace. What do you think about the principles of Buddhism as they relate to world peace?

Well the first thing is that you should realize yourself. How can peace be found without knowing yourself? In self-realization one finds the state of perfect equanimity. At this stage, you realize the origin of the phenomenal world and the intrinsic meaning of life.

You also come to possess the wisdom to discriminate correctly so that ultimately your mind is not disturbed by events taking place around you. In other words, one is able to live one's life comfortably and composedly without worries or anxiety. So when human beings come to know themselves as they really are, meaningless disputes will cease, and there will be peace.

Yes, you are correct. I think this is basically Wonhyo's principle of mutual interpenetration and all-inclusiveness. The power of returning to the origin rather than dividing and analyzing; this is what Buddhism is really about. I agree with your idea that world peace will be attained when the idea that all people possess the Buddha nature, which is the seed of realization, is established. So in this regard I completely agree with you.

There is no investigation of the person who is doing the dividing and analyzing in the Western philosophical and scientific tradition. In other words, there is no question of who the 'I', the person doing the analyzing, is. On the other hand, as I indicated before, Buddhism, being concerned with returning to the origin, investigates the 'I'. This is the salient feature of Buddhism. Nevertheless we now belong to the scientific and technical age. So we need to consider carefully how to effectively communicate the ideas of Buddhism in order to make Buddhism relevant to the modern world.

I feel that Buddhism in Korea won't become relevant to modern society merely through the reorganization of its institutions. The spreading of the Buddhist message to the rest of the world will only take place when the prevailing thinking changes. So when the education of Buddhist monks improves in quality, then we'll see the proliferation of the Buddhist ideal.

Humans are not born out of choice, but it is possible to control one's destiny to a degree. This can be achieved by controlling one's mind. This is the most important teaching of the Buddha. If I can control my mind, then my destiny can be changed. Through Zen practice and Yombul (mantra repetition) karma is dissolved and so one's destiny will naturally be altered. Just as a film director can edit the film he works with, destiny can be controlled when one realizes the self. Isn't the essence of Wonhyo's teachings of 'Harmonization' and the practice of 'No Obstacle' all about controlling one's own action and not discriminating against others?

As human beings we need desperately to eliminate our selfishness and consider the welfare of all living beings, including the planet itself, if we are to survive as a species. The planet is being crippled by our own uncontrolled pollution. As an example of this, everyday we face the issue of how to dispose of our garbage. So what is the Buddhist approach to dealing with these kinds of mundane issues?

You have a very good point. I think we need to adopt the Zen Buddhist idea of not wasting even a single grain of rice. If we live with this ethic then naturally we'll be able to find a sustainable solution to the issues of food and the elimination of waste matter. In the absence of such an approach it is unlikely that we'll be able to reverse the crippling damage that we are inflicting on our own planet. At the same time we need to train our own minds. Purity and restraint within our own selves will lead naturally to the solution of the mundane problems we face in the material world.

It seems that those with genuine spiritual understanding will have to assume many roles and do many things in this age. Only if Buddhists assume the mantle of responsibility in this way, can we avert the inevitable disaster being brought on by modern life. Technological civilization with its mechanized industrial structures has gradually been consuming the humanity of the individual. I think that for those brought up in the theistic social and religious traditions of the West, the spirit and culture of Zen Buddhism will bring a fresh impetus.

Of course what you say is correct. We need to perfect ourselves first, and at the same time we should endeavor to transmit the Buddhist teachings to our neighbors. This is the way to benefit not only our own country but also society at large, and the whole world. No matter how much science develops, it will never be able to fathom the secrets of consciousness itself. So ultimately, through empirical scientific investigation, the understanding of the human being is impossible. The human being is a composite entity of both body and mind. Consequently the intrinsic desire for the improvement of life can only be fulfilled through the spiritual life. One of the main tenets of Zen Buddhism is that the individual must experience and affirm the truth for himself.

It might just be that the significance of Zen to the modern age will be to enable the individual to find the wisdom to live his/her life resourcefully and confidently. The spiritual world cannot be seen or affirmed through the physical eyes. It can only be comprehended through the mental eye of realization. Buddhism is useful in that it can help people internalize the problems of this modern age through their individual experience. We must come to realize that civilization will not be saved by God or Buddha, but by our selves. With the help of the wisdom of Zen Buddhism we can recover our humanity and lead meaningful lives in harmony with each other and the world we inhabit. So we must all become Bohdisattvas in order to save the world.

Biography

Seung Sahn Sunim was born in Sunch'on, South P'yong'an province in 1927. He became a monk at Magok-sa in 1947, and received Inka from Zen master Kobong at Sudok-sa in 1949. He became the head monk of Hwagye-sa in 1958 and the first president of the Bulgyo Shinmun (Buddhist newspaper). He began his international Buddhist propagation work by opening Hongbop-won in Japan in 1966, and since that time he has established Zen centers in Hong Kong, the U.S., Canada, Brazil, Europe, and Singapore. He is now Senior Zen master of Hwagye-sa and a member of the presiding council of the Chogye order.

Zen Masters and Temples of Korea

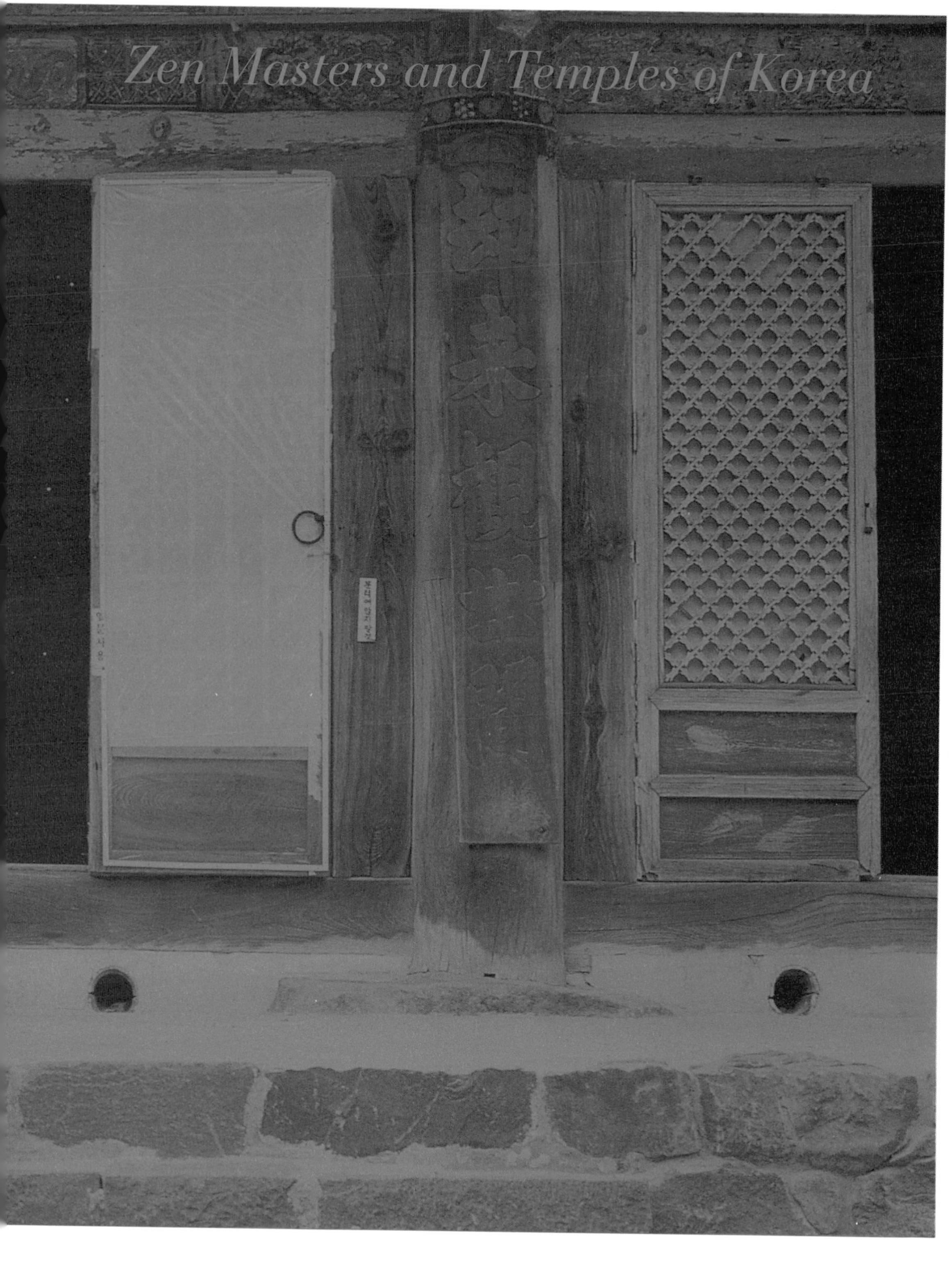

NOTES

1 | T ang Dynasty 618-907 AD.

2 | For the sake of consistency, the word Zen has been used throughout the text, except where the context dictates otherwise. Zen is the Japanese transliteration of the Chinese word Ch an which is derived from the Indian word, Dhyana meaning meditation or absorption. The Korean transliteration of the word is Son .

3 | The Fourth Patriarch was Tao-hsin. According to Zen history, the Zen lineage can be traced all the way back to the Buddha Sakyamuni. The Zen lineage is referred to as the Transmission outside the Scriptures . According to tradition, the first patriarch in India was Mahakasyapa. One day the Buddha was giving a discourse on Mt. Grdhrakuta when suddenly he held up a flower. Everyone was silent: only Mahakasyapa smiled. Sakyamuni said, I have the eye of the true teaching, the heart of nirvana, the true aspect of non-form. It cannot be expressed in words but is especially transmitted outside the teachings. This transmission I have given to Mahakasyapa. In all there were 28 Patriarchs in India. Bodhidharma then brought the teaching to China and is regarded as the First Patriarch of the Chinese Zen School. The Second Patriarch was Hui-k o, the Third Patriarch Seng-ts an, the Fourth Patriarch Tao-hsin, the Fifth Patriarch Hung-jen and the Sixth Patriarch Hui-neng. (See Appendix 1.)

4 | The Sixth Patriarch Hui-neng (638-713) was the dominant figure of Chinese Zen; he introduced the concept of sudden illumination and ushered in the period known as the Golden Age of Zen in China. His biography and teachings can be found in The Altar Sutra of Hui-neng .

5 | The Nine Mountains Schools were: 1. the Kaji Mountain School, 2. the Songju Mountain School, 3. the Tongni Mountain School, 4. the Shilsang Mountain School, 5. the Bongni Mountain School, 6. the Sagul Mountain School, 7. the Saja Mountain School, 8. the Huiyang Mountain School and, 9. the Sumi Mountain School. With the exception of the Huiyan Mountain School, which traces its origins back to the Fourth Patriarch Tao-hsin, and the Sumi Mountain School, which was derived from the Ts ao-tung (J: Soto) line, all the Korean Nine Mountains Schools originated from the first-generation successors of Ma-tsu Tao-i (709-788) and therefore technically predate the establishment of the Five Houses.

6 | The so-called Golden Age of Zen in China lasted until the Hui-cheng persecutions of Buddhism (842-845) and saw the development of the Five Houses of Zen. These were: The House of Kuei-shan, the House of Lin-chi (J: Rinzai), the House of Ts ao-tung (J: Soto), the House of Yun-men and the House of Fa-yen. During the Sung Dynasty (960-1279), these were merged so that only the house of Lin-chi and the House of Ts ao-tung remained.

7 | The Nine Mountain Sects were merged into the single Chogye Zen Sect in 1356 by T aego Po u (1301-82). T aego received transmission from the Chinese Master Shih-wu, an 18th-generation successor of Lin-chi I-hsuan (d.866). It is for this reason that many present day Korean masters trace their lineage back through T aego to the Chinese Lin-chi sect.

8 | See footnote 40.

9 | Kim, Taljin, Korean Zen Poems, Ancient and Modern, volume 2, p.205.

10 | Hyo Bong Oh, Wonhyo s Theory of Harmonization, p.242.

11 | One of the important texts of Mahayana Buddhism, attributed to Asvaghosa, a renowned Buddhist Master who lived in India during the 1st Century AD.

12 | The Avatamsaka Sutra (Flower Garland Sutra) is one of the main texts of Mahayana Buddhism. (C: Hua-yen, K: Hwaom). Symbolically through parables, narratives and images, it describes the Buddhist metaphysical view of the universe and emphasizes the doctrines of identity and interpenetration.

13 | Adapted from the P yowon-jip (Collection of Master P yowon) in The Collection of Korean Buddhist Texts 2, p.366a.

14 | Chong-Ik Lee, <Wonhyo ui Sasang> (Wonhyo s Fundamental Philosophy), pp.81,116.

15 | Cheol-u Mok, ed., <Wonhyo Jeonjip> Wonhyo s Complete Collection, p.51.

16 | Kwanseum Bosal in Korean and Guan-yin in Chinese.

17 | Another of the central Mahayana texts (see Glossary).

18 | Chae, Taek-su, The Unified Shilla Period, The History and Culture of Buddhism in Korea, p.92.

19 | A 73-character summary of the essence of the teaching of the Hwaom Sutra, written by Uisang whilst he was in China.

20 | Translated by Yi, Chi-kuan, Hwa-om Philosophy, Buddhist Thought in Korea, pp.82-84.

21 | P ang Yun of Hsiang-chou (?-811), studied under Masters Shih-t ou His-ch ien (700-790) and Ma-tsu (709-788), the fathers of the two main lines of Zen during the T ang period. After attaining illumination, he threw all his possessions in the river. It is said that the entire family were enlightened. As he wrote:

I have a son who has never been married;

Neither has my daughter.

We all come together and talk about no-birth. (From The Transmission of the Lamp, chapter 8).

22 | Literally, the three baskets .

23 | Ma-tsu Tao-I (709-788), Patriarch Ma , along with Bodhidharma and the Sixth Patriarch Hui-neng, was one of the dominant figures of early Zen. He promoted the dynamic Zen of Hui-neng and was the first to make use of shouting to shock his students into awakening. It is said that he was a man of extraordinary vigour who had the bearing of an ox and the gaze of a tiger . At the height of his fame, more than 800 students were studying under him at his monastery. By the time that he passed away he had given transmission to 139 disciples.

24 | Hsi-tang Chih-tsang (748-834), was one of the three outstanding disciples of Ma-tsu along with Pai-chang and Nan-ch uan.

25 | Pai-chang Huai-hai (720-814) established the rules for Zen monks. He also introduced the practice of working in the fields. This made the Zen monasteries largely self-sufficient and independent of state support, which enabled them to survive the political and social turmoil that was to come in succeeding years. Pai-chang s famous saying was: A day without work is a day without food.

26 | The brilliant and enigmatic Nan-ch uan P u-yuan (748-835) was one of the three main successors of Ma-tsu. He was the abbot of a large community of monks and is best remembered as the teacher of Chao-chou (778-897), who inherited his Dharma.

27 | Adapted from Chae, Taek-su, Son Philosophy, Buddhist Thought in Korea, p.31.

28 | Dates unknown.

29 | Adapted from Chae, Taek-su, Son Philosophy, Buddhist Thought in Korea, p.32.

30 | Probably because of his noble background Muyom was far better received than Toui, who returned to Shilla before him. He was appointed as National Teacher at the courts of both Kings Kyongmun (r.861-875) and Hongang (r.875-886), and died in 888 AD. On his death he was given the posthumous title of Master Nanghye-hwasang, meaning, Great Bright Wisdom .

31 | The other is Bong am-sa (see p.90).

32 | Suh, Yoon-kil, Buddhism in the Koryo Dynasty, Buddhist Thought in Korea, p.126.

33 | Ibid., p.123.

34 | Huai-hui Ch ang-ch ing (755-815) was another of Ma-tsu s numerous disciples. A well-known saying of this master was: In the midst of myriad phenomena the solitary body of the Dharmakaya reveals itself. He was often quoted by Master Fa-yen Wen-i (885-958), the founder of the House of Fa-yen, whose teaching style emphasised the existence of the fundamental reality within the phenomenal world.

35 | Today nothing at all remains of Bongnim-sa. Somewhat poignantly, the site of this important temple was turned into a graveyard in the early 20th Century. The stupa to Master Chingyong was moved to Kyungbok Palace in 1919.

36 | Seo, Kyung-bo, A Study of Korean Zen Buddhism Approached through the Chodangjip, p.151.

37 | Yueh-shan Wei-yen (745-828) was one of the two main successors of Shih-t ou Hsi-ch ien (700-790).

Shih-t ou means Stone-head , because of the meditation hut that he built on top of a large flat rock and in which he lived for twenty years. The two main lines of Chinese Zen during the T ang period were derived from Shih-t ou and Ma-tsu, who were contemporaries.

38 | Seo, Kyung-bo, A Study of Korean Zen Buddhism Approached through the Chodangjip, pp.151-152.

39 | The Hui-cheng persecution of Buddhism in China (842-845) was a result of the resentment felt by the Confucian and Taoist factions over the growing material prosperity and power of the Buddhist temples. Emperor Wu-tsang (r.841-846) was strongly influenced by prominent Confucian and Taoist ministers at his court. In 845 AD it was alleged that a Buddhist monk had had a liaison with a court lady and had made her pregnant. Using this as an excuse, an edict was issued by the court that resulted in the destruction of all the major Buddhist temples and establishments of the day. Around 260,000 monks and nuns were forced to return to secular life. Many Buddhist statues and pagodas were destroyed and sutras were burnt. Temple bells were melted down and lands seized by the state. This effectively put an end to the Golden Age of Buddhism in China. Zen, with its ethos of self-sufficiency, managed to survive by retreating to the mountains. Nonetheless, Buddhism was never again to have the support and popularity that it enjoyed during this period.

40 | Seo, Kyung-bo, A Study of Korean Zen Buddhism Approached through the Chodangjip, p.154.

41 | Nangwon Kaech ong became a monk at the age of twenty. After practising asceticism alone for three years on Gold Mountain, he met an old man who advised him that there was a saint living on Mt. Sagul. You should go there to learn the truth, he said. When Nangwon arrived there, Pomil greeted him and said, What took you so long? I ve been waiting for you all this time! Nangwon passed away at the age of ninety-six. Seo, Kyung-bo, A Study of Korean Zen Buddhism Approached through the Chodangjip, p.154.

42 | Nanggong Haenjok studied the Avatamsaka Sutra at Haein-sa when he was young. In 870 AD he went to Mt. Wu-tai in China, the mountain of Manjusri. He received Inka from Master Shishuang Ch ing-chu and returned to Korea in 884 AD. He attracted more than five hundred disciples.

43 | About Nan-ch uan (748-834) see footnote 26.

44 | The free-spirited Chao-chou Ts ung-shen (778-897?) was the successor of Nan-ch uan. It is said that he lived to the age of 120. After his enlightenment he spent many years traveling around visiting the monasteries of other teachers. As a result there are many exchanges involving Chao-chou recorded in the Zen literature. He only settled down at the age of eighty at Kuan-yin Monastery, where many students came to meet him; however, he was never interested in establishing his own lineage.

45 | Seo, Kyung-bo, A Study of Korean Zen Budd-hism Approached through the Chodangjip, p.186.

46 | The direct and independent Tung-shan Liang-chieh (807-869) was the founder of the Tsao-tung House.

His teacher was Yun-yen (782-841), a second-generation successor of Shih-t ou. The Tsao-tung House is noted for the expedient teaching of the doctrine of the Five Positions of Prince and Minister .

47 | Seo, Kyung-bo, A Study of Korean Zen Buddhism Approached through the Chodangjip, pp.197-198.

48 | Near Kaesong, the capital of the Koryo Dynasty, located in present-day North Korea. No longer extant.

49 | Nagabe Kazuo, Study of Master I-Hsing.

50 | Choson-sach al-saryo (Historical Materials on Korean Temples) 2, p.377.

51 | Adapted from, Suh, Yoon-Kil, Buddhism in the Koryo Dynasty, Buddhist Thought in Korea, p.121.

52 | Choson-sach al-saryo (Historical Materials on Korean Temples) 2, p.202.

53 | Tien-tai, the Chinese school of Buddhism which bases its teachings on the Lotus Sutra.

54 | K: Hwaom

55 | C: Ch an, K: Son, J: Zen

56 | Kim, Taljin, Korean Zen Poems, Ancient and Modern, in two volumes, p.38.

57 | Pojo-kuksa-pi-myong (Inscription of National Master Pojo), in Pojo-chonso (Collection of Master Pojo), p.420. (Trans. R.E.Buswell).

58 | Buswell, The Korean Approach to Zen; The Collected Works of Chinul, p.24.

59 | Ibid., p.27.

60 | Songgwang-sa, representing the Sangha (community of monks) is one of the Three Treasures temples. The other two are T ongdo-sa, which represents the Buddha, and Haein-sa, which represents the teachings.

61 | Buswell, The Korean Approach to Zen; The Collected Works of Chinul, p.28.

62 | Chinul, Sushim-kyol (Secrets on Cultivating the mind), in Collection of Master Pojo, p.39. (Trans. R.E.Buswell).

63 | Chinul probably found this doctrine in the writings of T ang Zen Master Zongmi (780-841).

64 | Buswell, The Korean Approach to Zen, p.144.

65 | In developing this aspect of his philosophy, Chinul drew on the writings of Li Tongxuan (635-730), an obscure 8th Century Chinese commentator on the Avatamsaka Sutra.

66 | The Hwadu (C: Hua-t ou) is a term that refers to a special type of question used as a meditation tool to still the mind. In Korea it is often used as a synonym for Kongan (J: Ko-an); however, technically the two are different. Kongan (public case) refers to an entire situation/exchange, usually a dialogue between a Zen master and student, whilst Hwadu refers to just the central issue.

67 | By the mid-Sung Period, Zen had become polarized into two main styles: the Silent Illumination Zen of the Tsao-tung (J: Soto) school, and the Kongan practice of the Lin-chi (J: Rinzai) school. Ta-hui Tsung-kao (1089-1163) warned against the heterodoxy of the popular Silent-Illumination Zen as advocated by Hung-chih Cheng-chueh (1091-1157) and vigorously promoted the use of the Kongan. He further refined the method of Kongan study by introducing the Hua t ou (K: Hwadu).

68 | A 19th/20th Century Chinese successor of Ta-hui, Zen Master Hsu-yun, explained the Hwadu as follows: There are many Hwadus, such as: All things return to the one; where does the one return to? What was your original face before you were born? Who am I? What is this? Who is repeating the Buddha s name? etc. But what is the Hwadu? Literally it means word head . Word is the spoken word and head is that which precedes word. Before a word is spoken it is a Hwadu or ante-word. So that which is called Hwadu is the moment before a thought arises. As soon as a thought arises, it becomes a hua-wei or word tail. The moment before a thought arises is called the unborn. That void which is neither disturbed nor dull, and neither still nor moving, is called the unending. The unremitting turning of the light inwards on oneself, instant after instant, and exclusive of all else, is called looking into the Hwadu or taking care of the Hwadu. When one looks into the Hwadu the most important thing is to give rise to a doubt. Doubt is the crux of the Hwadu. For instance when one is asked: Who is repeating the Buddha s name? everybody knows that he himself repeats it. But is it repeated by the mouth or the mind? If the mouth repeats it, why doesn t it do so when one is asleep? If it is the mind that repeats it, then what does the mind look like? As mind is intangible one is not clear about it. Consequently some slight feeling of doubt arises about WHO. This doubt should not be coarse; the finer it is the better. At all times and in all places this doubt should be looked into unremittingly, like an ever flowing stream, without giving rise to a second thought. From: Lu Kwan Yu, Ch an and Zen Teaching Vol.1., p.23.

69 | (C: Wu) Meaning: nothing , empty or no .

70 | From: The Collection of the Sayings of Ta-hui (C: Ta-hui Yu-lu), T. 1998, Vol. 47, p.901.

71 | Buswell, The Korean Approach to Zen, pp.32-33.

72 | Ibid., p.145.

73 | Kim, Taljin, Korean Zen Poems, Ancient and Modern, in two volumes, p.66.

74 | Lee, Young-Ja, Ch ont ae Philosophy, Buddhist Thought in Korea, p.151.

75 | Suh, Yoon-kil, Buddhism in the Koryo Dynasty, The History and Culture of Buddhism in Korea, p.158.

76 | Lin-chi I-hsuan (d.866), the successor to the Dharma of Huang-po Hsi-yuan (d.850) was another of the giants of the Zen pantheon. An imposing figure who is best remembered for his blows and shouts, he was at the same time a humanistic thinker who enjoyed dialectics. The focal point of his philosophy was the unconditioned true man of no rank . The lineage which he founded became the most influential and long lasting of all the Chinese Zen schools.

77 | The name Chogye is derived from the mountain in China where the Sixth Patriarch Hui-neng resided.

78 | Seo, Kyung-bo, A Study of Korean Zen Buddhism Approached through the Chodangjip, p.328.

79 | Ibid., p.329.

80 | Ibid., p.329.

81 | T aego-hwasang-orok (The Records of Master T aego),1, in The Whole Collection of Korean Buddhist Texts, 6.

82 | Seo, Kyung-bo, A Study of Korean Zen Buddhism Approached through the Chodangjip, p.101.

83 | Kim, Taljin, Korean Zen Poems, Ancient and Modern, in two volumes, p.160.

84 | Paegun means White Cloud .

85 | Sayings of Master Paegun, in Whole Collection of Korean Buddhist Texts 6, p.649.

86 | Upon his return to Korea, Paegun stayed mainly at Ankuk-sa, Shinkwan-sa and Chonyang-am, all of which were located in present day N. Korea. Later he stayed on Mt. Mangsan at Kimp o and passed away at Chiam-sa. None of these temples remain today.

87 | Sayings of Master Paegun, in Whole Collection of Korean Buddhist Texts 6, p.656.

88 | See Ch onch uk-sa.

89 | Master Hyegam (1249-1319) was a 10th generation successor of Master Chinul. He was abbot of Songgwang-sa and national teacher.

90 | Seo, Kyung-bo, A Study of Korean Zen Buddhism Approached through the Chodangjip, p.126.

91 | There is a story that illustrates his friendship with the king. One day the king came to visit Muhak at Hoeam-sa. Dismissing his attendants, he complained to Muhak that because of his position as king, he could not even laugh freely anymore. He said to Muhak, Let s dispense with formality and have some fun. Muhak said, All right, Your Highness, you make the first joke.
The king said, Muhak, you look like a pig to me!
Muhak bowed and said, Thank you. Your Highness looks to me like the Buddha on Vulture Peak. The king was perplexed by this reply and asked him what he meant.
Muhak replied, Through pig s eyes you only see pigs; through Buddha s eyes you only see Buddhas!

At this the king burst out laughing.

From: Seo, Kyung-bo, A Study of Korean Zen Buddhism Approached through the Chodangjip, p.127.

92 | Seo, Kyung-bo, A Study of Korean Zen Buddhism Approached through the Chodangjip, p.128.

93 | Ibid., p.116.

94 | Kim, Taljin, Korean Zen Poems, Ancient and Modern, in two volumes, p.211.

95 | Yi, Chi-kuan, Hwa-om Philosophy, Buddhist Thought in Korea, p.110.

96 | Seo, Kyung-bo, A Study of Korean Zen Buddhism Approached through the Chodangjip, p.103.

97 | Kim, Taljin, Korean Zen Poems, Ancient and Modern, in two volumes, p.122.

98 | The Houndang-jip in 3 Vols: poems and prose.

99 | Seo, Kyung-bo, A Study of Korean Zen Buddhism Approached through the Chodangjip, p.338.

100 | Ibid., p.340.

101 | Sosan Ch onghojip, p.27.

102 | Ibid., p. 29.

103 | Mirror of Zen <Songa Kwigam> No.34.

104 | Sosan Taesa, Mirror of Zen, translated by Mark Mueller, p.8.

105 | According to legend, the room emitted a mysterious fragrance for twenty-one days after his passing.

106 | In the shrine room there are portraits of Sosan and his two disciples, Samyong and Cheo-yeong, who led the monk militia.

107 | From Mirror of Zen (Songa Kwigam).

108 | Kim, Taljin, Korean Zen Poems, Ancient and Modern, in two volumes, p.274.

109 | The event is recorded as follows: One day P yonyang was late returning to the temple, so Sosan asked him where he had been. P yonyang said that he had climbed the peak to find wild mushrooms. Then Sosan asked whether he had seen any mountain lions up on the peak. P yonyang just kept silent. Then suddenly he roared and leapt forward and bit Sosan. Surprised, Sosan grabbed his Zen stick and tried to chase him away, but P yonyang was too quick. Sosan burst out laughing and exclaimed, Fantastic, fantastic; today I ve been beaten! The next day Sosan gathered all his students in the main hall and ascended the Dharma platform. Be careful, he said, there is a wild mountain lion loose in the Diamond Mountains. Look out or you ll get bitten! Already yesterday I was mauled. Saying this, he pounded his Zen staff on the platform and left the hall. From: Seo, Kyung-bo, A Study of Korean Zen Buddhism Approached through the Chodangjip, pp.352-353.

110 | Kim, Taljin, Korean Zen Poems, Ancient and Modern, in two volumes, p.352.

111 | Ibid., p.304.

112 | At the time of reconstruction, a five-storey pagoda was erected containing murals of the life of Sakyamuni Buddha. It is the oldest and tallest wooden pagoda in Korea today. There also used to be a hall that contained a 39-foot (12-meter) high Maitreya statue that dated back to the Shilla period. It was dedicated by Priest Chinp yo in 776 AD. In 1872, during the latter years of the Choson Dynasty when Buddhism was being severely repressed, this statue was melted down by Prince Regent Taewon-gun so that coins could be minted to fund the reconstruction of Kyongbuk Palace. A 25-meter tall bronze Maitreya statue weighing 160 tons was erected in 1989 on the same site to replace it.

113 | No longer extant.

114 | Kim, Taljin, Korean Zen Poems, Ancient and Modern, in two volumes, p.372.

115 | Ibid., p.390.

116 | The Chiri Mountains area is today the most famous tea-growing region in Korea.

117 | The legend goes that after Master Chinpyo, who is said to have had special powers, returned from China, he had a vision in which Maitreya appeared and gave him a book on fortune-telling together with a book of monks rules. This fortune-telling book became the principle authority on the subject in Korea. After this, Master Chinpyo was often invited by King Kyongdok (r.742-765) to the royal palace to give discourses on geomancy.

118 | The focal point of the temple is the Maitreya Buddha Hall. Enshrined in the hall is a 39-foot (12-meter) tall golden statue of the future Buddha Maitreya flanked by his two attendants.

119 | He wrote a book called, An Introduction to the Five Principles of Zen which enjoyed considerable popularity at the time.

120 | Located in present-day N. Korea.

121 | Kim, Taljin, Korean Zen Poems, Ancient and Modern, in two volumes, p.468.

122 | Ibid., p.500.

123 | Seo, Kyung-bo, A Study of Korean Zen Buddhism Approached through the Chodangjip, 133.

124 | Yong means shadow and san means mountain.

125 | Seo, Kyung-bo, A Study of Korean Zen Budd-hism Approached through the Chodangjip, p.134.

126 | Ibid., pp.361-2.

127 | Adapted from Mok, Jeong-Bae, The History and Culture of Buddhism in Korea, p.242.

128 | Ibid., p.245.

129 | Adapted from Sok Do-ryun, Korea Journal, February 1, 1965, p.31.

130 | Seo, Kyung-bo, A Study of Korean Zen Budd-hism Approached through the Chodangjip, p.366.

131 | Adapted from Mok, Jeong-Bae, The History and Culture of Buddhism in Korea, p.243.

132 | Seo, Kyung-bo, A Study of Korean Zen Buddhism Approached through the Chodangjip, p.397.

133 | Mu Soeng, Thousand Peaks, p.175.

134 | Seo, Kyung-bo, A Study of Korean Zen Budd-hism Approached through the Chodangjip, p.398.

135 | Ibid., p.399.

136 | Son, Wonbin, Kun Sunim, p.140.

137 | Ibid., p.141.

138 | Ibid., p.142.

139 | Ibid., p.142.

140 | See Buswell, The Korean Approach to Zen; The Collected Works of Chinul.

141 | Adapted from Seo, Kyung-bo, A Study of Korean Zen Buddhism Approached through the Chodangjip, p.399.

142 | Adapted from Mok, Jeong-Bae, The History and Culture of Buddhism in Korea, p.255.

143 | Adapted from Mok, Jeong-Bae, The History and Culture of Buddhism in Korea, p.248.

144 | The five skandas are the physical body.

145 | Adapted from Seo, Kyung-bo, A Study of Korean Zen Buddhism Approached through the Chodangjip, p.400.

146 | Adapted from Mok, Jeong-Bae, The History and Culture of Buddhism in Korea, p.249.

147 | Seo, Kyung-bo, A Study of Korean Zen Budd-hism Approached through the Chodangjip, p.371.

148 | Ibid., p.374.

149 | Sok Do-ryun, Korea Journal, April 1, 1965, p.18.

150 | All these experiences enabled him to perceive the stagnation and backwardness that characterized Buddhism in Korea at that time. The external world was evolving fast, yet Korea at the turn of the 20th Century was loathe to participate. In 1909 he wrote a critique called, On the Revitalization of Korean Buddhism . He felt that if Buddhism was to survive the onslaught of Japanese colonization that he saw coming, Korean Buddhism needed to reform itself from within. His main contention was that Buddhism could only really come to life through the realization that the essence of Buddhism lay not in the institutional fabric of the temples, but rather in each individual s personal life.

151 | Adapted from Mok, Jeong-Bae, The History and Culture of Buddhism in Korea, p.236.

152 | Kusan Sunim, The Way of Korean Zen, Stephen Batchelor, ed., p.43.

153 | Adapted from Seo, Kyung-bo, A Study of Korean Zen Buddhism Approached through the Chodangjip, p.405.

154 | Kusan Sunim, The Way of Korean Zen, Stephen Batchelor, ed., p.44.

155 | While meditating such experiences sometimes happen. You could say it was a certain opening of the mind s eye. It was the transition over a difficult step that enabled me to first gain admittance to the door... perhaps you could call it an initial breakthrough. It showed that my practice was progressing well. Ibid., p.45.

156 | Ibid., p.46.

157 | Ibid., p.47.

158 | Ibid., p.47.

159 | Ibid., p.50.

160 | Ibid., p.50.

161 | Ibid., p.145.

162 | Son, Wonbin, Kun Sunim, p.161.

163 | Ibid., p.162.

164 | Ibid., p.167.

165 | Ibid., p.179.

166 | Ibid., p.179.

167 | Ibid., p.181.

168 | Ibid., p.212.

169 | Ibid., p.223.

170 | Ibid., p.239.

171 | Ibid., p.240.

172 | Ibid., p.243.

173 | Ibid., p.269.

174 | Ibid., p.270.

175 | Zen Master Jinjae teaches at Hae-un Jong-sa, near Pusan.

176 | Son, Wonbin, Kun Sunim, p.271.

177 | In order to discourage all but the most serious seekers, the prerequisite for meeting him was to perform three thousand prostrations. This could take anywhere between 15-24 hours to complete. Asked the reason for this he said: "I always tell people that they'll gain nothing by seeing me and that they should look for Buddha instead. But they come anyway. So I have them prostrate 3,000 times. They are not for me however; I have them prostrate for others. You see something happens to people after doing 3,000 prostrations for all forms of life. They have an inexplicable change of heart..."

178 | From a conversation with Pop-jong Sunim, Chung-Ang Daily Newspaper, Jan. 1, 1982, translated by Brian Barry.

179 | The 8th Level of Consciousness, called the Storehouse Conciousness.

180 | Annual Address, Full Moon of the 6th Lunar Month, 1981, Haein-sa, translated by Brian Barry.

181 | Sempto Monthly Magazine, May, 1983.

182 | Mu Soeng, Thousand Peaks, p.194.

183 | . Seo, Kyung-bo, A Study of Korean Zen Buddhism Approached through the Chodangjip, pp.372-373.

184 | Mu Soeng, Thousand Peaks, p.195.

185 | Ibid., p.198.

186 | Ibid., p.204.

GLOSSARY

Am: Hermitage in Korean.

Amitabha: The Buddha of infinite light who presides over the Western Paradise otherwise known as the Pure Land.

Avatamsaka Sutra: The Flower Garland Sutra (C: Hwa-yen, K: Hwaom) of Mahayana Buddhism. Considered to be the crowning achievement of Mahayana Cosmology.

Avalokitesvara: (C: Guan-yin, K: Kwanseum Bosal, T: Chenrezig) The God/Goddess of Compassion in the Buddhist pantheon. Usually depicted with eleven heads and one thousand arms, all of which are used in the dispensation of aid to suffering beings. Avalokitesvara is an attendant of the Buddha Amitabha.

Awakening: The realization or perception of one s self-nature; initial enlightenment attained upon the inception of prajna.

Bodhi: Enlightenment.

Bodhidharma: The Indian meditation master who, according to legend, brought Zen Buddhism to China circa. 520 AD. The 28th Patriarch of Zen in India and the First Patriarch of Chinese Zen. He is said to have dwelled in seclusion at Shaolin facing the wall for nine years awaiting a successor.

Bodhisattva: A being who aspires to perfect enlightenment in order to save others. Considered to be the highest aspiration of Mahayana Buddhism. Important Bodhisattvas in the Mahayana pantheon are Avalokitesvara who personifies compassion and Manjusri who personifies wisdom.

Buddha: Literally, the one who is enlightened or the one who knows .

Bosal: Bodhisattva in Korean.

Buddha-nature: One s ultimate reality or true identity.

Ch'an: See Zen .

Ch'ont'ae: (C: Tien-tai) The eclectic Buddhist School which originated in China and based its teachings on the Lotus Sutra. It also incorporated the meditative Ch an practices as well as the more esoteric teachings derived from Tantric Buddhism.

Chukpi: The hollowed-out bamboo rod which is used to strike practitioners who are dozing during meditation. Also used in the Korean tradition to signify the beginning and end of the meditation period.

Dharani: Mantra

Dharma: A Sanskrit term meaning, depending on the context, the teachings of Buddhism, the universal law or phenomena/matter.

Dharmadhatu: The realm of reality . The universe in its totality; the reality underlying the world of perception.

Dharmakaya: The body of reality; the ultimate ground of all existence.

Dharma-nature: The absolute essence of all things.

Diamond Sutra: (Skt: Vajracchedika prajnaparamita-sutra) One of the essential Mahayana texts belonging to the Perfection of Wisdom Series which focuses on expounding the Doctrine of Emptiness.

Emptiness: (Skt: Sunyata) According to Madhyamaka philosophy, all things including phenomena, perceptions, mental constructs etc. are merely the result of the interplay of causal conditions and have no stable, inherent, independent identity. One of the core concepts of Buddhism.

Feng-shui: Literally means: take wind, get water . The traditional Chinese science of reading the energies of the earth s landscape.

Five precepts: Buddhists are supposed to refrain from the following five vices: 1) taking life, 2) taking what is not given, 3) sexual misconduct, 4) lying and 5) consuming intoxicants.

Ganges: The most sacred river in India, along the banks of which many saints and yogis have resided.

Ghosa: Layman.

Heart Sutra: One of the shortest of the Mahayana Sutras belonging to the Perfection of Wisdom series. Emphasis is on the teaching of emptiness.

Hwadu: (C: Hua-t ou) A term which refers to a special type of question used as a tool to still the mind. Literally it means head of speech and denotes the place whence thoughts arise. In Korea it is often used as a synonym for Kongan (J: Ko-an) however technically the two are different. Kongan (public case) refers to an entire situation/exchange, usually a dialogue between Zen master and student, whilst Hwadu refers to just to the central issue.

Hwaom: (C: Hwa-yen , Skt: Avatamsaka) See Avatamsaka.

Inka: Recognition of understanding or attainment.

Karma: The law of cause and effect.

Kido: Literally energy way . Refers to the religious practice of chanting or reciting dharanis (mystical formulas).

Kongan: (J: Ko-an) See Hwadu .

Kosa: Layman.

Lotus Sutra: The Sutra on the Lotus of the Good Dharma . One of the most popular and influential discourses of Mahayana Buddhism delivered by the Buddha on Vulture Peak. The text dates back to the 1st Century AD and is set in verse and elaborated in prose. The Sutra supposedly has magical powers in its own right, and great merit accrues for those who extol and disseminate it.

Mahayana: Great Vehicle . The Mahayana ideal emerged some two or three-hundred years after the death of the historical Buddha. Central to this vision is the concept of the Bodhisattva who aspires to salvation in order to help other sentient beings. The most distinguishing feature of Mahayana Buddhism is therefore its advocacy of the Bodhisattva as the vehicle to liberation. This is in contrast to the arahant ideal of Hinayana (Small Vehicle) Buddhism.

Maitreya: (K: Miruk) The Buddha destined to be born on earth in a future era.

Manjusri: (K: Munsu Bosal) The Bodhisattva of Wisdom. Often depicted holding a sword which he uses to cut through the veil of ignorance.

Mantra: A mystical formula repeated by the religious devotee.

Mind: In Zen this term is used in two ways; firstly to denote the ultimate reality and secondly to denote mind as it is ordinarily understood.

Mokt'ak: A hollow, fish-shaped wooden instrument which is struck rhythmically to maintain tempo during chanting.

Mu: (C: Wu) emptiness/nothing.

Nirvana: The state of perfection reached upon cessation of the defilements (greed, aversion and delusion).

Original face: One s self-nature.

Patriarch: A realized master through whom the lineage of the Zen tradition has been passed down from the Buddha Sakyamuni to the present day.

Pojo: Posthumous name given to Master Chinul of Songgwang-sa.

Prajna: Transcendental wisdom.

Pure Land: A heavenly realm in the Buddhist cosmology ruled over by Amitabha Buddha. This Pure Land is a place for heavenly rebirth which anyone can reach merely by reciting the name of Amitabha.

Rinzai: Japanese transliteration of Lin-chi (C). Refers both to the Chinese Zen master and his school.

Sa: Temple in Korean.

Samadhi: A concentrated state of being where the mind is unaffected by externals.

Samantabhadra: The Bodhisattva who personifies selfless action.

Samsara: Illusion.

San: Mountain in Korean.

Sangha: The community of Buddhist monks and nuns.

Sarira: Small crystallized pieces of varying sizes often found in the ashes of monks and meditation practitioners after cremation. They are believed to be an indication of spiritual maturity and are often worshiped as sacred relics.

Sakyamuni: (Gautama) The historical Buddha who lived in India around 500 BC.

Son: See Zen .

Soto: Japanese name for the Ts ao-tung sect, one of the original Five Houses of Chinese Ch an.

Stele: A memorial stone bearing an inscription.

Stupa: A dome-shaped monument in memory of a holy person.

Sudden Teachings: The doctrine that truth can be apprehended suddenly without any preliminary practices.

Sunim: The Korean title for monks.

Sutra: The Sanskrit term for a discourse given by the Buddha.

Tathagata: An epithet for the Buddha. Literally, One who abides in suchness .

Ten stages: The ten stages of Bodhisattva development as described in the Avatamsaka Sutra.

Tao: See way .

Transmission: The invisible mind-to-mind transference of the mind seal from master to elected successor. Usually signifies the student s qualification to be a holder of the master s lineage.

Vairocana: The name of the Cosmic Buddha whose body symbolically represents the phenomenal universe.

Vimalakirti: An enlightened layman who lived in India at the time of the Buddha and whose teachings are recorded in the Vimalakirti-nirdesa-sutra.

Vinaya: The code of rules for monks.

Void: See emptiness .

Way: (C: Tao) A term derived from Taoism which refers to both the path of the aspirant and the ultimate principle of the universe.

Yebul: Short ceremony lasting around half an hour held every morning at 3.30 am and every evening at 6.30 pm in Korean temples.

Zen: (C: Ch an, K: Son) Derived from the Sanskrit term Dhyana, meaning concentration or meditative absorption. Also refers to the tradition which began in China with the arrival of Bodhidharma from India in the 6th Century AD. Additionally it is sometimes used to refer to the quality of a master s insight or attainment.

BIBLIOGRAPHY

Buddhist Culture in Korea. International Cultural Foundation, ed. Seoul: Sisa-yong-sa Publishers, 1982.

Buddhist Thought in Korea, ed. The Korean Buddhist Research Institute. Seoul: Dongguk University Press, 1994.

Buswell, Robert E. Jr. trans. *The Korean Approach to Zen; The Collected Works of Chinul.* Honolulu: University of Hawaii Press, 1983.

Dumoulin, Heinrich, *Zen Buddhism a History Vol.1 India and China.* James W. Heisig and Paul Knitter, trans. London: Collier Macmillan Publishers 1988.

Chang, Chung-Yuan, *Original Teachings of Ch'an Buddhism: Selected from the Transmission of the Lamp.* New York: Vintage Books, 1971.

Cho'nt'ae Thought in Korean Buddhism, ed. Korean Buddhist Research Institute. Seoul: Dongguk University Press, 1999.

Cleary, Christopher, trans. *Swampland Flowers: The Letters and Lectures of Zen Master Ta Hui.* New York: Grove Press, 1977.

Dictionary of Korean Buddhist Temples. Seoul: Bulgyo Sit ae sa, 1985.

Han, Chung Kwan, *Kyongho; Zen Master.* Seoul: Hankilsa, 1999.

History and Culture of Buddhism in Korea, ed. The Korean Buddhist Research Institute. Seoul: Dongguk University Press, 1993.

Iryon, *Samguk Yusa: Legends of the Three Kingdoms of Ancient Korea.* N. Grafton, K. Mintz and Tae-Hung Ha, trans. Seoul: Yonsei University Press, 1972.

Kang, Kon Ki, *Songgwang-sa.* Seoul: Taewonsa, 1994.

Kim, Po Hyon, *Pusok-sa.* Seoul: Taewonsa, 1995.

Kim, Taljin, *Korean Zen Poems, Ancient and Modern, in two volumes.* Seoul: Yolhwadang, 1984.

Korean Buddhism, Chogye Order, ed. Song Wol Ju. Seoul: Kum Sok, 1995.

Korean Buddhist Biographical Dictionary. Seoul: Bulkyo Sit ae sa, 1990.

Kusan Sunim, *Nine Mountains: Kusan the Meditation Master.* Private publication: Songgwang-sa, 1978.

Kusan Sunim, *The Way of Korean Zen*, Stephen Batchelor, ed. New York: Weatherhill, 1985.

Lee, Kyong-hee, *World Heritage in Korea.* Seoul: Samsung Foundation, 1997.

Lu Kwan Yu, *Ch'an and Zen Teaching Vol.1.* London: Rider, 1988.

Mu Soeng, *Thousand Peaks: Korean Zen Tradition and Teachers.* Berkeley: Parallax Press, 1987.

Oh, Young Bong, *Wonhyo's Theory of Harmonization.* PhD. Dissertation, New York University, 1988.

Shin, Young Hun, *Architecture of Historic Temples.* Seoul: Taewonsa, 1989.

Seo, Kyung-bo, *A Study of Korean Zen Buddhism Approached through the Chodangjip.* (Ph.D. dissertation, Temple University, 1960; mimeographed reprint, Seoul, 1973.)

Seung Sahn, *Dropping Ashes on the Buddha: The Teaching of Zen Master Seung Sahn.* Stephen Mitchell, ed. New York: Grove Press, 1976.

Seung Sahn, *Only Don't Know: The Teaching Letters of Zen Master Seung Sahn.* San Francisco: Four Seasons Foundation, 1982.

Shim, Jae-ryong, *Korean Buddhism Tradition and Transformation;* Korean Studies Series 8. Seoul: Jimoondang Publishing, 1997.

Son Thought in Korean Buddhism, ed. Korean Buddhist Research Institute. Seoul: Dongguk University Press, 1998.

Son, Wonbin, *Kun Sunim.* Seoul: 1991.

Song-chol, *Echoes from Mt. Kaya,* translated by Brian Barry. Seoul: Lotus Lantern, 1987.

Sosan Taesa, *Mirror of Zen; A Korean Buddhist Classic,* translated by Mark Muller. Seoul: Chogye Order Publication, 1995.

T aego, *A Buddha From Korea; The Zen Teachings of T'aego,* translated by J.C. Cleary. Boston: Shambhala, 1988.

Wu, John C.H., *The Golden Age of Zen.* Taipei: United Publishing Center, 1975.

Genealogy of the Nine Mountains Zen Schools

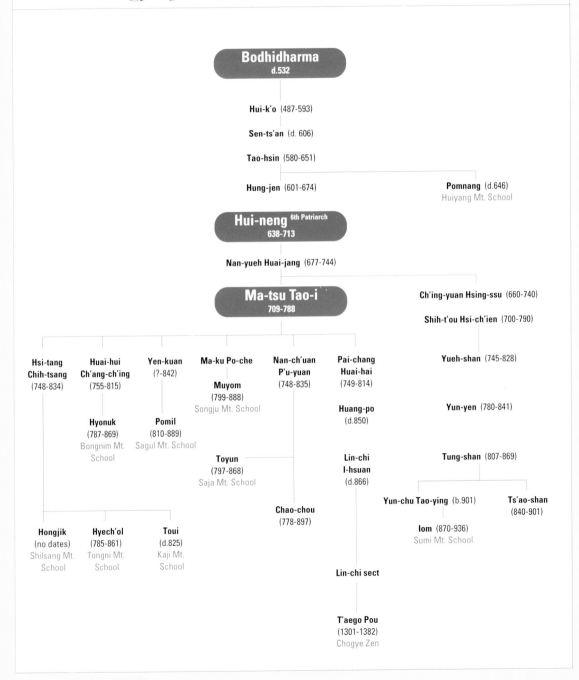

Bodhidharma
d.532

Hui-k'o (487-593)

Sen-ts'an (d. 606)

Tao-hsin (580-651)

Hung-jen (601-674)

Pomnang (d.646)
Huiyang Mt. School

Hui-neng 6th Patriarch
638-713

Nan-yueh Huai-jang (677-744)

Ma-tsu Tao-i
709-788

Ch'ing-yuan Hsing-ssu (660-740)

Shih-t'ou Hsi-ch'ien (700-790)

Hsi-tang
Chih-tsang
(748-834)

Huai-hui
Ch'ang-ch'ing
(755-815)

Yen-kuan
(?-842)

Ma-ku Po-che

Muyom
(799-888)
Songju Mt. School

Nan-ch'uan
P'u-yuan
(748-835)

Pai-chang
Huai-hai
(749-814)

Yueh-shan (745-828)

Huang-po
(d.850)

Yun-yen (780-841)

Hyonuk
(787-869)
Bongnim Mt.
School

Pomil
(810-889)
Sagul Mt. School

Toyun
(797-868)
Saja Mt. School

Lin-chi
I-hsuan
(d.866)

Tung-shan (807-869)

Chao-chou
(778-897)

Yun-chu Tao-ying (b.901)

Ts'ao-shan
(840-901)

Iom (870-936)
Sumi Mt. School

Hongjik
(no dates)
Shilsang Mt.
School

Hyech'ol
(785-861)
Tongni Mt.
School

Toui
(d.825)
Kaji Mt.
School

Lin-chi sect

T'aego Pou
(1301-1382)
Chogye Zen

Korean and Chinese Dynasties

Korean Dynasties		Chinese Dynasties
	206 BC-220 AD	Han
Shilla	57 BC-660 AD	
Koguryo	37 BC-668 AD	
Paekche	18 BC-660 AD	
	220-265 AD	Three Kingdoms
	265-420 AD	Jin (Tsin)
	420-580 AD	Southern and Northern
	589-618 AD	Sui
	618-907 AD	T'ang
Unified Shilla	660-935 AD	
	907-960 AD	Five Dynasties
Koryo	918-1392 AD	
	960-1280 AD	Sung
	1280-1368 AD	Yuan
	1368-1644 AD	Ming
	1644-1911 AD	Qing (Ching)
	1911-1949	Republic of China
Choson	1392-1910	

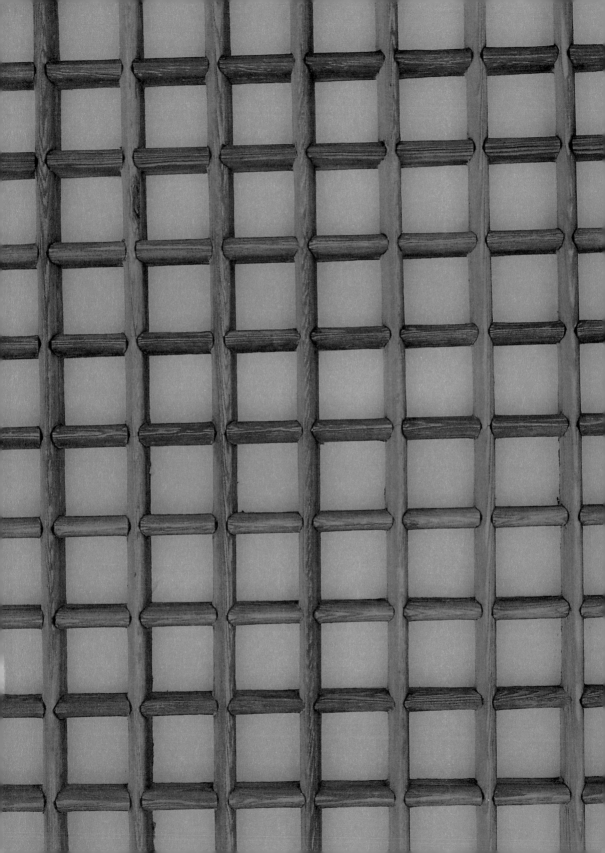

Zen Masters & Temples of Korea

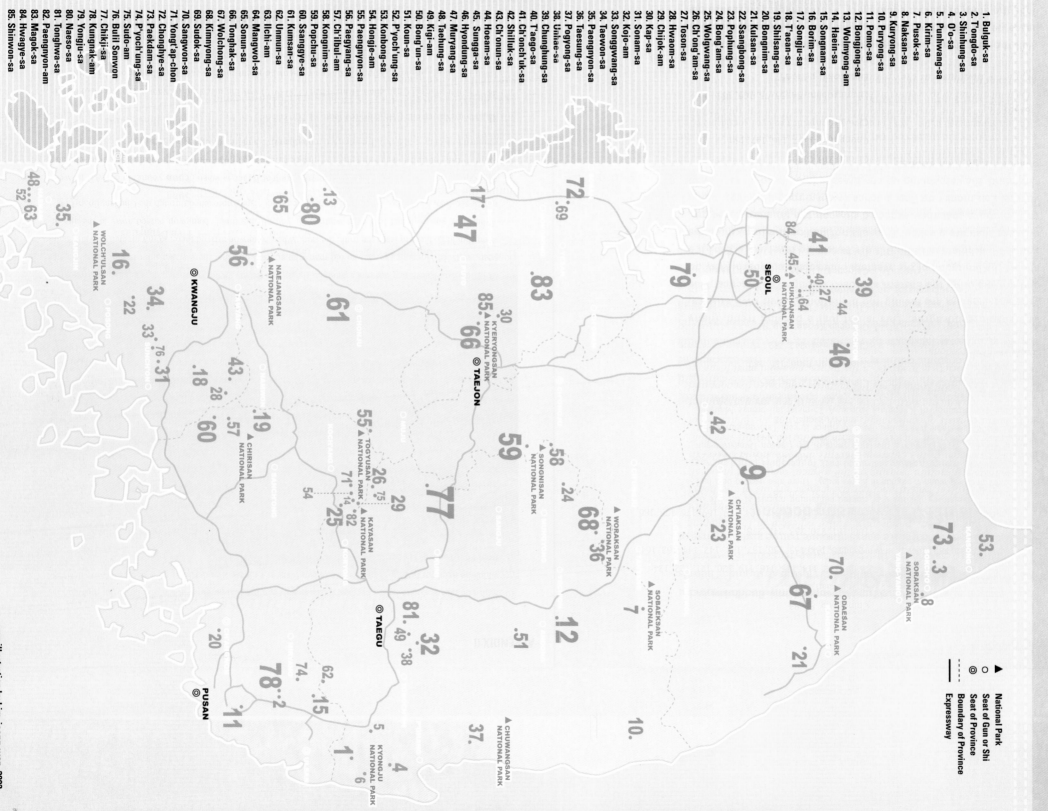

WOLCH'ULSAN
NATIONAL PARK

NAEJANGSAN
NATIONAL PARK

KWANGJU

KYERYONGSAN
NATIONAL PARK

TAEJON

SEOUL

PUKHANSAN
NATIONAL PARK

CH'IAKSAN
NATIONAL PARK

SOBAEKSAN
NATIONAL PARK

SORAKSAN
NATIONAL PARK

ODAESAN
NATIONAL PARK

SONGNISAN
NATIONAL PARK

WORAKSAN
NATIONAL PARK

CHIRISAN
NATIONAL PARK

TOGYUSAN
NATIONAL PARK

KAYASAN
NATIONAL PARK

CHUWANGSAN
NATIONAL PARK

TAEGU

PUSAN

KYONGJU
NATIONAL PARK

▲	National Park
○	Seat of Gun or Shi
◎	Seat of Province
- - - -	Boundary of Province
———	Expressway

map illustration by kim, jeong-won. 2002

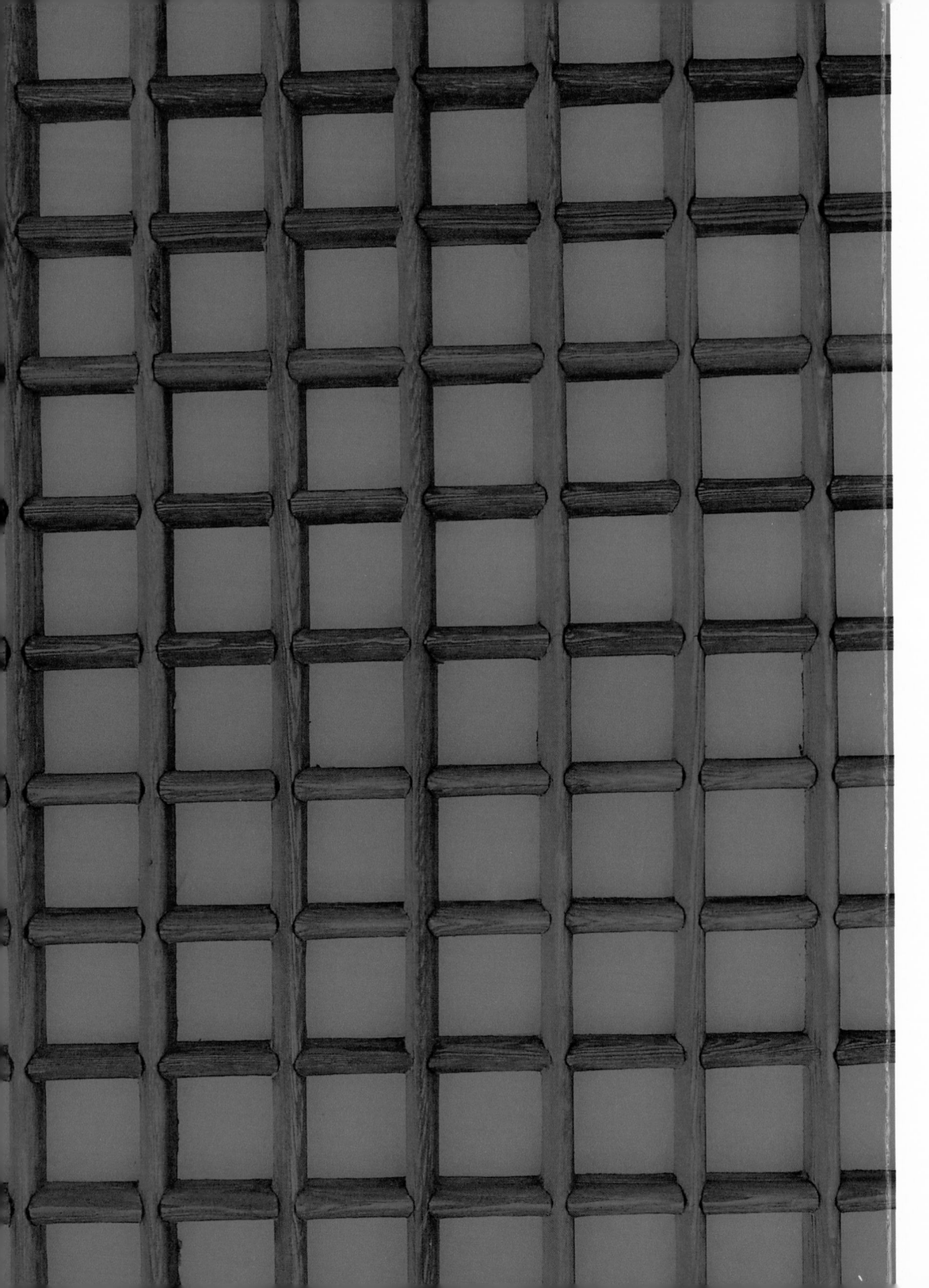

Romanization Table of Korean Temple Names

No.	McCune-Reischauer Romanization of Korean	New Romanization of Korean (issued on Aug. 4, 2000)	Korean
1.	Bulguk-sa	Bulguksa	불국사
2.	T'ongdo-sa	Tongdosa	통도사
3.	Shinhung-sa	Sinheungsa	신흥사
4.	O'o-sa	Oeosa	오어사
5.	Punhwang-sa	Bunhwangsa	분황사
6.	Kirim-sa	Girimsa	기림사
7.	Pusok-sa	Buseoksa	부석사
8.	Naksan-sa	Naksansa	낙산사
9.	Kuryong-sa	Guryongsa	구룡사
10.	Puryong-sa	Buryeongsa	불영사
11.	Pomo-sa	Beomeosa	범어사
12.	Bongjong-sa	Bongjeongsa	봉정사
13.	Wolmyong-am	Wolmyeongam	월명암
14.	Haein-sa	Haeinsa	해인사
15.	Songnam-sa	Seongnamsa	석남사
16.	Borim-sa	Borimsa	보림사
17.	Songju-sa	Seongjusa	성주사
18.	T'aean-sa	Taeansa	태안사
19.	Shilsang-sa	Silsangsa	실상사
20.	Bongnim-sa	Bongnimsa	봉림사
21.	Kulsan-sa	Gulsansa	굴산사
22.	Ssangbong-sa	Ssangbongsa	쌍봉사
23.	Pophung-sa	Beopheungsa	법흥사
24.	Bong'am-sa	Bongamsa	봉암사
25.	Wolgwang-sa	Wolgwangsa	월광사
26.	Ch'ong'am-sa	Cheongamsa	청암사
27.	Toson-sa	Doseonsa	도선사
28.	Hwaom-sa	Haweomsa	화엄사
29.	Chijok-am	Jijokam	지족암
30.	Kap-sa	Gapsa	갑사
31.	Sonam-sa	Seonamsa	선암사
32.	Kojo-am	Geojoam	거조암
33.	Songgwang-sa	Songgwangsa	송광사
34.	Taewon-sa	Daewonsa	대원사
35.	Paengnyon-sa	Baengnyeonsa	백련사
36.	Taesung-sa	Daeseungsa	대승사
37.	Pogyong-sa	Bogyeongsa	보경사
38.	Unhae-sa	Eunhaesa	은해사
39.	Chunghung-sa	Jungheungsa	중흥사

No.	McCune-Reischauer Romanization of Korean	New Romanization of Korean (issued on Aug. 4, 2000)	Korean
40.	T'aego-sa	Taegosa	태고사
41.	Ch'onch'uk-sa	Cheonchuksa	천축사
42.	Shilluk-sa	Silleuksa	신륵사
43.	Ch'onun-sa	Cheoneunsa	천은사
44.	Hoeam-sa	Hoeamsa	회암사
45.	Sungga-sa	Seunggasa	승가사
46.	Hyondung-sa	Heyondeungsa	현등사
47.	Muryang-sa	Muryangsa	무량사
48.	Taehung-sa	Daeheungsa	대흥사
49.	Kigi-am	Gigiam	기기암
50.	Bong'un-sa	Bongeunsa	봉은사
51.	Koun-sa	Gounsa	고운사
52.	P'yoch'ung-sa	Pyochungsa	표충사
53.	Konbong-sa	Geonbongsa	건봉사
54.	Hongje-am	Hongjeam	홍제암
55.	Paengnyon-sa	Baengnyeonsa	백련사
56.	Paegyang-sa	Baegyangsa	백양사
57.	Ch'ilbul-am	Chilburam	칠불암
58.	Kongnim-sa	Gongnimsa	공림사
59.	Popchu-sa	Beopjusa	법주사
60.	Ssanggye-sa	Ssanggyesa	쌍계사
61.	Kumsan-sa	Geumsansa	금산사
62.	Unmun-sa	Unmunsa	운문사
63.	Ilchi-am	Iljiam	일지암
64.	Mangwol-sa	Mangwolsa	망월사
65.	Sonun-sa	Seonunsa	선운사
66.	Tonghak-sa	Donghaksa	동학사
67.	Wolchong-sa	Woljeongsa	월정사
68.	Kimnyong-sa	Gimnyongsa	김룡사
69.	Sudok-sa	Sudeoksa	수덕사
70.	Sangwon-sa	Sangwonsa	상원사
71.	Yongt'ap-chon	Yongtapjeon	용탑전
72.	Chonghye-sa	Jeonghyesa	정혜사
73.	Paekdam-sa	Baekdamsa	백담사
74.	P'yoch'ung-sa	Pyochungsa	표충사
75.	Sudo-am	Sudoam	수도암
76.	Bulil Sonwon	Buril Seonwon	불일선원
77.	Chikji-sa	Jikjisa	직지사
78.	Kungnak-am	Geungnakam	극락암
79.	Yongju-sa	Yongjusa	용주사
80.	Naeso-sa	Naeseosa	내소사
81.	Tonghwa-sa	Donghwasa	동화사
82.	Paengnyon-am	Baengnyeonam	백련암
83.	Magok-sa	Magoksa	마곡사
84.	Hwagye-sa	Hwagyesa	화계사
85.	Shinwon-sa	Sinwonsa	신원사

INDEX

EMPTY HOUSE

First edition, 2002

Published by Eastward Publications, Inc.
34-20 Jamwon-dong, ICM BD #402
Seocho-gu, Seoul 137-904, Korea
Tel: 82-2-3445-2775
Fax: 82-2-3445-2776
Web: www.eeastward.com
E-mail: morning@eeastward.com

Printed in KOREA

Cover and text design by Moon, Jisook
Printing & binding by 冊工房工冊

ISBN 89-952155-4-2 03220